GEOLOGY ENCYCLOPEDIAS

THE MINERAL ENCYCLOPEDIA

BY JILL C. WHEELER

Encyclopedias

An Imprint of Abdo Reference
abdobooks.com

TABLE OF CONTENTS

A WORLD OF TREASURES

Minerals are the building blocks of most of Earth's rocks. Geologists have identified more than 6,000 different minerals. Minerals come in many shapes, textures, colors, and sizes. Sometimes a mineral contains a single chemical element. Other times, it includes a combination of elements.

All minerals share several characteristics. Minerals are solid. Each sample of a specific mineral features the same chemical formula. The crystal structure of a mineral is arranged in a precise, consistent pattern. Minerals are created by geological processes rather than the biological processes that create plants and animals.

Geologists group minerals based on the chemicals they contain. Native element minerals, such as gold or silver, contain atoms of a single element. An atom is the smallest unit of any substance, or matter.

Other minerals contain multiple kinds of atoms. These minerals are classified by the presence of specific elements in them. Sulfide minerals contain sulfur atoms, while sulfate minerals have both sulfur and oxygen atoms. Halide minerals contain chlorine or fluorine atoms. Oxide minerals contain oxygen atoms, while carbonates have both carbon and oxygen atoms. Phosphates contain phosphorus and oxygen atoms. Silicates are the largest mineral class. They have both oxygen and silicon atoms.

Minerals also differ in their color and level of hardness. These differences play a role in how minerals are used.

Minerals such as diamonds are valued for their hardness. They are used for drill bits or as gemstones. Minerals such as lithium and cobalt are valued for their use in modern batteries. Some of the most valuable minerals today had little to no value when they were first discovered. Recently discovered minerals may likewise require more research to identify specific uses.

HOW MINERALS FORM

Rocks and minerals that form from cooling magma or lava are known as igneous.

Minerals begin as atoms of one or more chemical elements. Usually, these atoms are floating randomly in a liquid such as water or molten rock. The atoms become minerals when they join together in specific patterns to form crystals. Changes in temperature and pressure, along with evaporation, cause atoms to come together.

Some minerals begin deep inside Earth in pools of superheated molten rock called magma. The heat causes the atoms in the magma to move quickly. As the magma breaks through Earth's surface, it becomes lava and begins to cool. This causes the atoms in the lava to slow down and connect to other atoms. The resulting neat, repeating patterns of atoms are minerals. This process is called crystallization.

Some minerals form when the water around their atoms evaporates. This process is called precipitation. Over time, the atoms can grow into crystals. White deposits on faucets and showerheads are caused by the same process. Calcium and magnesium in tap water are left behind as the water evaporates.

Mineral precipitation often occurs along the shores of salty bodies of water, such as the Kuyalnik Estuary in Ukraine. The salt from the water crystallizes.

MINERAL TRANSFORMATION

Minerals can also crystallize when hot substances other than molten rock cool down. Hot water can change some minerals from solid to liquid. This can be seen when pouring salt into a pot of boiling water. The salt dissolves in the water. But once the solution begins to cool, the minerals cannot remain dissolved. They begin to form crystals in a variety of geometric shapes, including needles, prisms, and even perfect cubes. Many mineral gemstones are formed when hot water under

Quartz is a common silicate mineral known for its crystal formations. Some types of quartz, such as amethyst, citrine, and rose quartz, are used as gemstones.

Earth's surface cools down. This creates beautiful crystals such as quartz.

A mineral also can change into another mineral when exposed to heat and pressure. This process is called metamorphism. It happens when extreme heat and pressure rearrange the atoms in a mineral. Soft pencil lead and hard diamonds are both made of carbon atoms. Their chemical structures are different due to the conditions under which they were formed.

Temperature, pressure, and chemical composition all play a role in a mineral's formation. In this way, minerals offer important clues about what happened in Earth's past. Minerals can be found underground, in caves, beneath the sea, and in plain sight on Earth's surface.

Minerals can take millions of years to form naturally. In the meantime, people make some valuable mineral gemstones in laboratories. These synthetic minerals are produced using scientific techniques that mirror natural mineral-forming processes. Precision equipment can create lab-grown minerals in anywhere from a few weeks to a few months.

GEOLOGIC TIMESCALE

The geologic timescale measures periods in Earth's history. People use it to understand changes in the planet and the atmosphere. It also gives a timeline for life on Earth. The scale begins with Earth's formation more than 4.5 billion years ago. It stretches into the present day. The scale is divided into eons, eras, periods, and epochs. There have been four eons in Earth's history. The first three were the Hadean, Archean, and Proterozoic. Together, they make up the Precambrian Era.

Some minerals formed in outer space before Earth existed. Other minerals are as old as Earth. The oldest known minerals found on the planet are tiny zircon crystals. These are believed to be from the Hadean Eon, when Earth began to form. They are around four billion years old. Most of Earth's minerals were formed during its first 250 million years.

All of Earth's minerals came from elements found in objects that fell from space. These included meteorites and asteroids. The elements were first contained in an ocean of molten rock. The melting and solidifying of this rock ocean further mixed these elements into minerals. Many surface minerals developed around 2.3 billion years ago. This coincided with the development of an oxygen-rich atmosphere created by ancient bacteria in the Proterozoic Eon.

More than 80 percent of minerals required water to form. Most iron-containing ores formed when iron-rich ocean water was present about 1.8 billion years ago. Late Cenozoic Era glaciers created deposits of gold, diamonds, and other minerals more than one million years ago.

EON	ERA	PERIOD	EPOCH	MYA*
Phanerozoic	Cenozoic	Quaternary	Holocene	0.01
			Pleistocene	2.6
		Neogene	Pliocene	5.3
			Miocene	23.0
		Paleogene	Oligocene	33.9
			Eocene	56.0
			Paleocene	66.0
	Mesozoic	Cretaceous		145.0
		Jurassic		201.3
		Triassic		251.9
	Paleozoic	Permian		298.9
		Pennsylvanian		323.2
		Mississippian		358.9
		Devonian		419.2
		Silurian		443.8
		Ordovician		485.4
		Cambrian		541.0
Proterozoic Archean Hadean	Precambrian			2500
				4000
				4600

*Million Years Ago

BASTNÄSITE

Bastnäsite is Earth's most plentiful source of rare earth elements (REEs). These are metallic elements with special magnetic and electrical properties. The mineral is named after the Bastnäs Mine in Sweden, where it was found in 1838. Bastnäsite ranges from pale yellow to reddish brown, and it often has a glassy luster. Luster is the way light interacts with a mineral's surface. Bastnäsite is a semisoft mineral that is slightly softer than regular glass.

The Bastnäs Mine is in Västmanland, Sweden. In the early 1800s, cerium was discovered at the site. Bastnäsite is a source of this mineral.

Bastnäsite deposits have been found in the United States, China, and Madagascar.

RARE METAL FROM THE STARS

Bastnäsite can contain a metallic REE called europium. Scientists suspect that this unusual substance is created by dead stars crashing together in outer space. These collisions produce large amounts of silver, gold, and platinum. They may also produce a small amount of europium. Europium was once used to create the red colors in bulky, old-fashioned television displays.

RARE EARTH ELEMENTS

There are 17 REEs, including cerium, europium, lanthanum, and neodymium. In addition to their magnetic and electrical properties, REEs can also have catalytic properties. REEs are used to make magnets and devices such as video displays. China is the world's leading producer of REEs. These elements are rarely found in concentrated deposits. This makes them difficult and expensive to extract. Their rarity has led to an increased focus on using REEs wisely and recycling them whenever possible.

Bastnäsite is a critical mineral for modern lifestyles. The REEs it holds are used to make vibration motors in cell phones and magnets in speakers and microphones. Bastnäsite is found worldwide. It is mined primarily in China and in Mountain Pass, California.

BORAX

Borax, which is typically white to pale gray in color, is a versatile mineral. It dissolves in water easily. People have used it for cleaning purposes since ancient times. Today, many people still use cleaning, laundry, and insect control products that contain borax. People who work with metal may use borax in welding and soldering processes. The borax helps keep contaminants out of newly melted metal. Borax can also be used as a plant nutrient in farming. It is sometimes used to make stronger glass and ceramic products. Borax itself is roughly as hard as a human fingernail.

BORN IN THE SALT FLATS

Borax is a combination of water and the elements boron, sodium, and oxygen. The mineral typically forms in dry climates through the evaporation of water that is rich in boron salts. Borax deposits are often found in dry lake beds or salt flats. California's dry Searles Lake is one major source of borax. Other borax-producing locations include China, Chile, Argentina, and Turkey.

Borax is often used in household products such as laundry soaps, stain removers, and detergents.

CALCITE

Calcite is one of nature's most common building materials. Invertebrate marine organisms use calcite in seawater to create shells and coral reefs. Calcite is a key ingredient in limestone, marble, and cement too. It is composed of calcium, carbon, and oxygen.

Calcite is a soft mineral, rating 3 on the Mohs scale. It forms and dissolves easily. Calcite is primarily made of the chemical compound calcium carbonate. This compound is a source of the element calcium, which is important for plant and human nutrition. People use lab-produced calcium carbonate as a dietary calcium supplement. Calcium carbonate can help calm upset stomachs too.

Calcite's ability to neutralize acids means it can reduce the acidity of soils. Mineral hunters can use this acid neutralization ability to identify calcite-containing rocks. Rocks containing calcite bubble when exposed to acids such as vinegar.

FINDING CALCITE

Single calcite crystals can be almost transparent or white. But large

Calcium carbonate is a key ingredient in medications such as Tums, which treat indigestion and other stomach issues. The calcium carbonate helps reduce acids in the stomach.

collections of interlocking calcite crystals, or masses, can be white, off-white, or gray. Calcite forms in marine settings, hot springs, and large underground caves. Egypt, Malaysia, Turkey, Vietnam, and France are leading calcite producers.

THE MOHS SCALE

The Mohs scale was developed by German geologist Friedrich Mohs. It rates the hardness of minerals. The scale ranges from 10 to 1, with 10 being the hardest and 1 being the softest. Diamonds are a 10 on the Mohs scale, while corundum is a 9. Hard minerals such as these are often used for drill bits. A drill bit used on cement might have a Mohs rating of 8.5. The softest mineral is talc, which ranks 1 on the scale. This is softer than a human fingernail, which rates 2.5.

RATING MINERALS

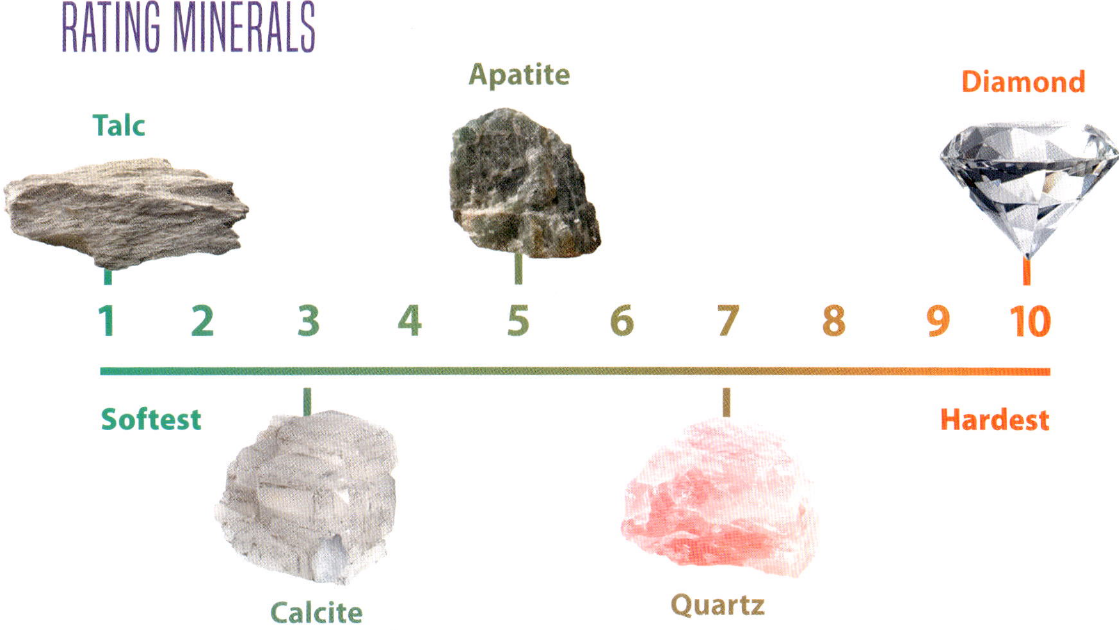

The Dolomites mountain range is home to large, layered dolomite formations such as the Tre Cime di Lavaredo, a group of three peaks.

DOLOMITE

Dolomite is a mineral composed of calcium, magnesium, carbon, and oxygen. It is typically found in sedimentary rocks that were once underwater. The Dolomites mountain range in the Italian Alps is made almost entirely of dolomite. The mineral and the mountain range were named after French geologist Déodat de Dolomieu. He was the first person to describe dolomite.

Crushed dolomite is an important ingredient in cement. Dolomite particles fill in the gaps between cement granules. This makes the cement smoother and easier to pack into corners and other small spaces. It also makes the material last longer.

Like calcite, dolomite is a source of calcium. Both calcite and dolomite are carbonate minerals. Powdered dolomite can be spread on farm fields to improve soil fertility. Dolomite is

also used in metalworking and in the production of glass and ceramic items.

A MASSIVE MINERAL

Dolomite is typically found in massive forms, such as the Dolomites mountain range. It is usually off-white, white, or gray in color. In crystal form, the mineral ranges from transparent to pink, or even brown or black if iron is present. Dolomite rates 3.5 to 4 on the Mohs scale. The mineral's softness makes it easy to use for industrial applications.

Dolomite can sometimes be found in clusters of tan or pink crystals.

MAGNESITE

Magnesite is a combination of magnesium, carbon, and oxygen. It is a refractory mineral, meaning it can remain stable under extreme heat. Bricks of this mineral are often used to build kilns because they can withstand temperatures of more than 2,000 degrees Fahrenheit (1,093°C). Steel, ceramics, and glass factories are primary users of refractory materials. Magnesite is also used for agricultural purposes. It is a source of the nutrient magnesium, which is good for plants.

Magnesite minerals sometimes have a lumpy texture.

MINERALS AND HUMAN HEALTH

Minerals can hurt or help human health. Some minerals contain toxic elements such as mercury, arsenic, or lead. Others have cancer-causing compounds such as asbestos. Still others contain radioactive elements that can cause sickness. But some minerals contain elements that are necessary for human, animal, and plant health. Calcium, iron, and magnesium are important for living things. Farmers may add these minerals to their fields to help plants grow. Plants take in minerals from the soil. When animals or humans eat the plants, they ingest these minerals. Humans also ingest minerals when drinking water and when eating animal-based products such as meat and milk.

Magnesite occurs in a range of colors. The mineral can be transparent, white, gray, yellow, brown, or pink. White magnesite can be easily cut and dyed to create inexpensive gemstones. Magnesite jewelry requires special care. This is because the mineral ranges from 3.5 to 5 on the Mohs scale.

METAMORPHIC ORIGINS

Magnesite is a carbonate mineral. Unlike most carbonate minerals, magnesite is not common in sedimentary rock. This is because it typically begins as a different type of mineral. Then it is transformed into magnesite under high heat and pressure. China, Turkey, Brazil, and Russia are leading magnesite producers.

Many factories use magnesite as a refractory material or process it into materials such as magnesium oxide. This material is used for a variety of industrial and agricultural purposes.

MALACHITE

Malachite has long been used as a pigment. This is because of the mineral's bright green color and resistance to fading. Today, malachite pigment remains visible in ancient Egyptian tomb paintings dating to 2600 BCE. It can also be seen in European artwork from the 1400s and 1500s CE. The mineral was once used as a source, or ore, of copper too. Modern malachite deposits are commonly used for jewelry and sculptures.

A DISTINCTIVE TARNISH

Malachite forms when copper-rich rocks are exposed to air and water. A similar process slowly turns copper roofs and statues green. Malachite can be found near copper deposits around the world, including in the southwestern United States. Malachite is a relatively soft mineral, with a Mohs rating of 3.5 to 4.

Malachite minerals sometimes have a banded appearance with swirling patterns of light green and dark green.

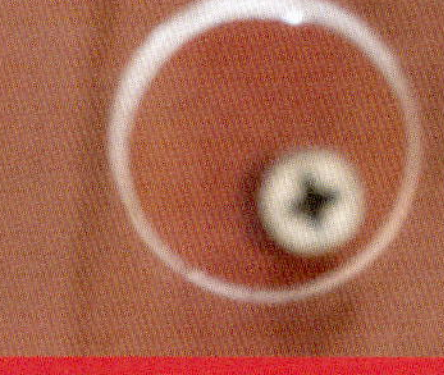

Ancient civilizations such as the Maya used malachite for decorative purposes. A Mayan funeral mask made of malachite was discovered in Mexico in 1994.

Fluorite is a source of the fluorine compound fluoride, which is commonly used in toothpaste.

FLUORITE

Fluorite, also known as fluorspar, is the primary source of the element fluorine. Companies add fluorine compounds to toothpaste and mouthwash to help prevent tooth decay. Fluorine can also be used to produce fluorine gas and hydrofluoric acid. These dangerous substances are used for industrial processes. Today, fluorite can be found all around the world. It is named for its ability to glow, or fluoresce, when exposed to ultraviolet light.

MINERAL WORKHORSE

Fluorite is a soft, colorless mineral. It is typically found in places where hot, mineral-rich fluids have evaporated or seeped into the ground. There, they cool and crystallize in cracks within existing rock beds. Fluorite deposits can be vibrant purple, blue, and green due to the presence of other minerals in these fluids. China and Mexico both produce large amounts of fluorite.

Fluorite has many commercial uses. It is used in lighting, as a flux in metal refining, and in ceramics and glass production. During World War II (1939–1945), scientists used fluorite to process uranium for the first atomic bomb.

DID YOU KNOW?

If something is changing, people may say it is "in flux." *Flux* means "flowing." Minerals such as fluorite are added to flux fluids, which are poured over other substances to capture and remove impurities.

Fluorite is a soft mineral with a Mohs rating of 4.

The Bonneville Salt Flats stretch about 12 miles (19 km) long. The salty expanse was once the site of Lake Bonneville, which dried up over time.

HALITE

Halite is commonly known as salt. This mineral is essential to cellular function in humans and animals. Most halite forms with the evaporation of seawater. It tends to be found alongside calcite, gypsum, and other minerals that commonly form through evaporation.

Halite is a soft mineral that is typically clear or white in color. The United States is home to several large halite deposits. These include the Great Salt Lake and the Bonneville Salt Flats in Utah. Another is the Louann Salt, a huge deposit that lies beneath parts of Louisiana and Texas.

SALT OF THE EARTH

Early humans used salt to disinfect wounds. Salt also helped people preserve meat before the invention of refrigeration. Some societies used salt as currency due to its high value. Humans' hunger for salt led to innovations in energy exploration. Miners drilling in salt domes, or underground halite deposits, found something unexpected. The domes held pockets of oil and natural gas. Salt is also a source of industrial chemicals such as chlorine and sodium hydroxide. In places with cold climates, salt is often spread on roadways to make snow and ice melt faster.

Table salt, which is often used in cooking and stored in saltshakers, is a purified form of halite.

Potash from sylvite is used in plant fertilizers worldwide. This makes sylvite an important mineral in the agricultural industry.

SYLVITE

Sylvite is an important source of the plant nutrient potassium, or potash. Potassium helps plants move water, nutrients, and carbohydrates within their tissues. A soft mineral, sylvite dissolves easily in water. It requires such a small amount of water to dissolve that it remains in liquid form until nearly all surrounding water has evaporated. Because of this, sylvite deposits often form on top of halite and other related minerals. Sylvite deposits are commonly found in dry lake beds and along the shores of salt lakes. The mineral can also be found near openings in Earth's crust called geothermal vents.

FINDING SYLVITE

Sylvite is primarily colorless or white. But it may also have light yellow, orange, and red hues. Sylvite deposits occur around the world. New Mexico is the leading producer of sylvite in the United States.

Sylvite, *pictured*, often looks similar to halite. But sylvite has a bitter taste, while halite tastes salty.

NATIVE ELEMENTS

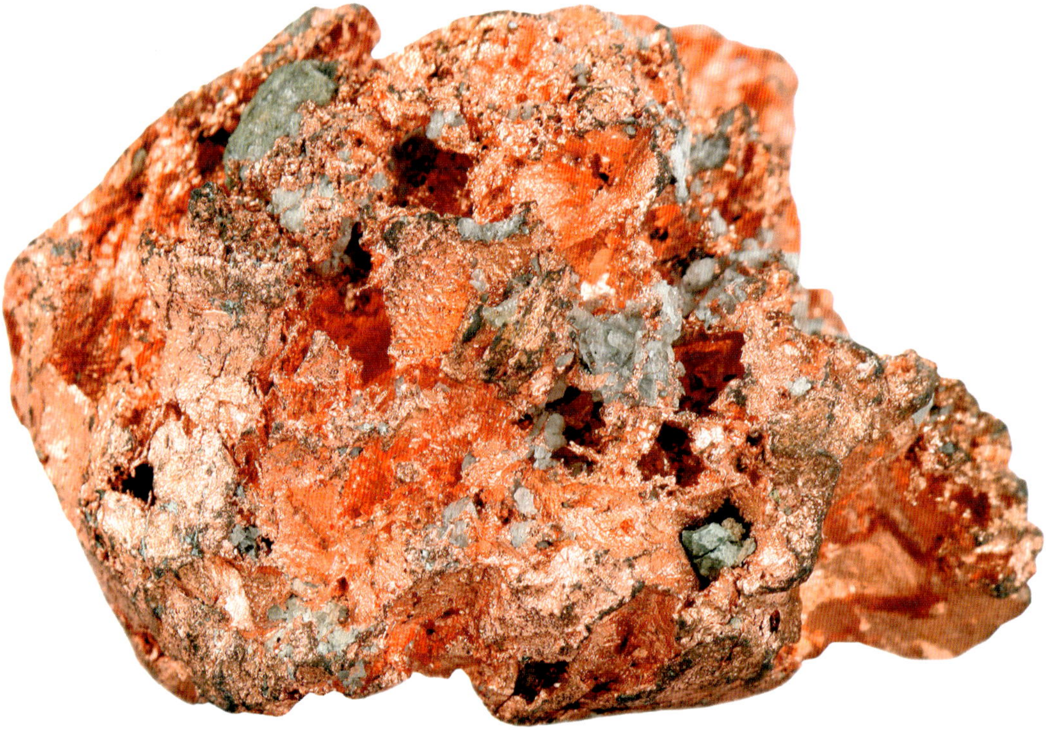

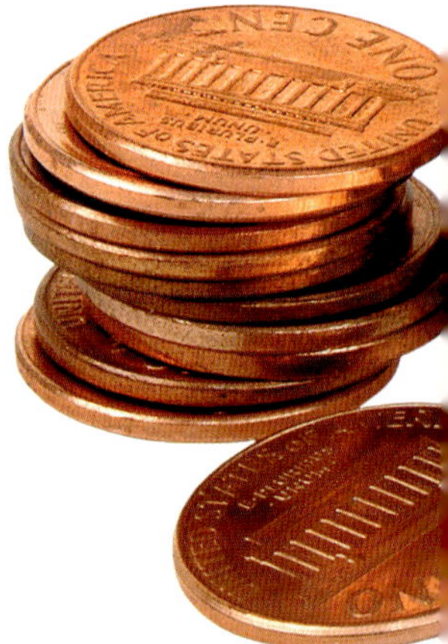

Native copper is known for its metallic luster. The mineral was one of the first metals used by ancient peoples.

COPPER

Copper is a soft mineral with a Mohs rating of 2.5 to 3. Its signature color is a reddish orange that changes to black or green when exposed to air. Pure copper is known as native copper. It can be found in nuggets in the ground. Copper-containing ores are often found in rocks of volcanic origin. Copper can be found near sedimentary rock layers too.

People have been using copper for roughly 10,000 years. Early humans used copper to make coins and decorative items. Later, people began mixing copper with other metals to create alloys. Alloys are mixtures of metals that are stronger, more flexible, or more resistant to rust than any single metal. One copper-based alloy is bronze. Early humans used this metal to make more durable weapons and tools. Today, copper is valued for its efficiency in conducting electricity.

ORES OF COPPER

Most copper comes from processing the copper-containing ores chalcopyrite and bornite. The United States is second only to Chile in the amount of copper it produces. Copper mines can be found in Arizona, New Mexico, Michigan, Utah, and Montana.

The first US pennies were made entirely of copper. Later, the coins were made of zinc with a copper coating.

GOLD

Gold is among the world's most popular minerals. This soft metal can be easily shaped and does not tarnish or discolor. Humans have been using gold for thousands of years, making it into coins, decorations, and jewelry.

Gold is rarely found in its pure form. It is most often found alongside silver. Areas with higher silver concentrations result in whiter shades of gold. Gold may be found within rocks such as granite and quartz. It also can be found in mineral deposits on Earth's surface. Today, China is the world's leading producer of gold, followed by Russia and Australia.

DON'T BE FOOLED

Gold is a heavy mineral. This means that it sinks in water. In the past, many people panned for gold in the sediment at the bottom of rivers and streams. The gold-colored mineral pyrite can also be found in these areas. Pyrite is nicknamed "fool's gold" because it is often mistaken for real gold.

Gold, *pictured*, is often more yellow in color than its look-alike pyrite. It is also softer than pyrite, rating 2.5 on the Mohs scale.

MINERAL DETECTIVES

Mineral exploration has changed greatly since the days of panning for gold in streams. Modern mineral detectives rely on high-tech equipment to find valuable minerals. Computers generate data-rich maps that help people identify potential deposits. Devices can use sound waves to create images of what lies below the surface. Orbiting satellites can detect mineral deposits based on how much solar radiation they reflect.

GRAPHITE

Graphite is a greasy mineral that ranges from silver gray to metallic black in color. It is among the softest minerals on Earth. Graphite easily leaves marks, making it a popular material for writing and drawing tools. Its name comes from the Greek word *graphein*, which means "to write."

Graphite is commonly mixed with clay to make pencil lead. It is also used to minimize friction between moving parts in machinery. Graphite's ability to withstand high temperatures makes it a popular material for lining furnaces. The mineral is used to produce lithium-ion batteries too.

RECYCLED ORGANICS

Most graphite forms as the result of heat and pressure on sedimentary rock. Organic material such as dead plants provides the carbon from which the graphite forms. Most graphite is found close to Earth's surface. The mineral occurs in many regions around the world, especially in Africa and Asia. China and Madagascar are the two leading producers of graphite.

Today, pencil lead is usually made of graphite mixed with clay.

DID YOU KNOW?

Traditional paper test forms often require test takers to use a #2 pencil. The graphite in this type of pencil reflects light from the test-scanning machine. This allows the machine to read the answers on the form.

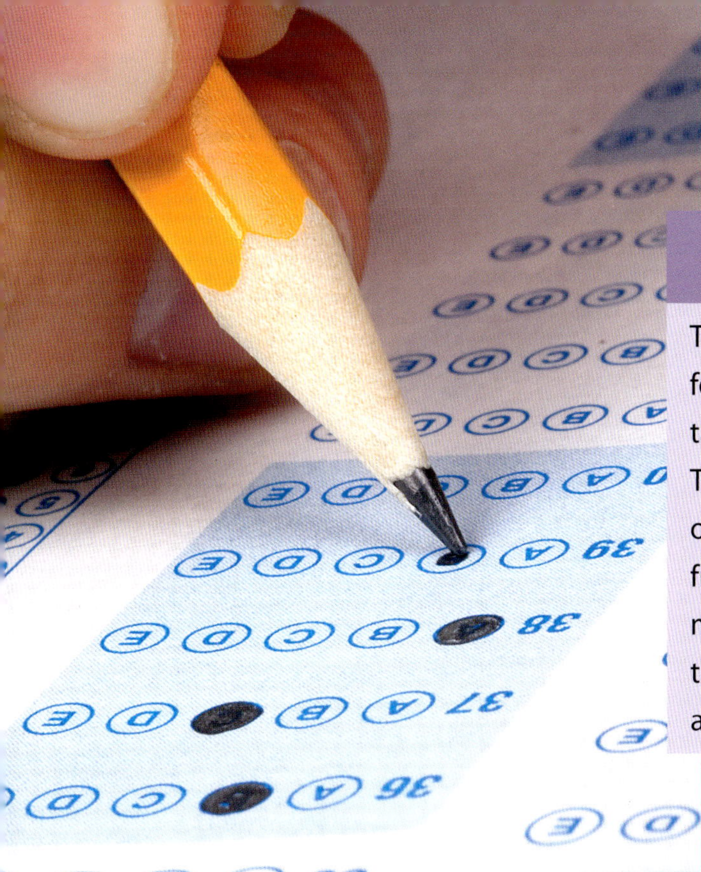

Graphite rates 1 to 2 on the Mohs scale.

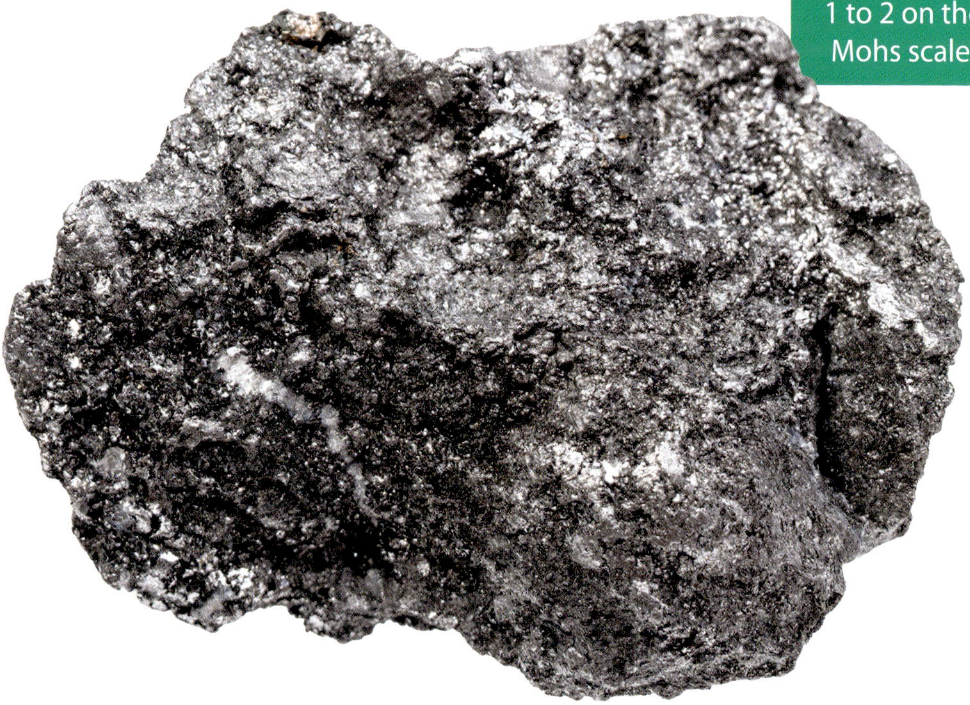

SULFUR

Sulfur is a soft yellow mineral and chemical element. When exposed to moisture in the air, it emits the smell of rotten eggs. Ancient societies used sulfur for medicine and insect control. Modern agriculture still relies on sulfur as an essential plant nutrient. Sulfur is also used to produce sulfuric acid, which is in a variety of chemical products. These include paint strippers, detergents, and dyes.

UNDERGROUND ORIGINS

Sulfur is among the most abundant chemical elements on Earth. It is commonly found in hot water that escapes Earth's crust through geysers and volcanoes. More concentrated sulfur deposits often form through the evaporation of seawater. The seawater forms the minerals gypsum and anhydrite. When gypsum and anhydrite are deeply buried in the ground,

Sulfur minerals are often powdery in texture and sometimes feature crystals.

Sulphur Caldron, an acidic hot spring at Yellowstone National Park, contains large amounts of sulfur.

bacteria alter those deposits to form sulfur. This process can result in large pockets of hydrogen sulfide gas in the same places as oil and natural gas deposits. Today, these deposits are used to meet the modern demand for sulfur. Sulfur is used for a variety of chemical and industrial purposes. China is the world's leading producer of sulfur, followed by the United States.

BOEHMITE

Boehmite is one of three key minerals in bauxite, an aluminum ore. Boehmite is a little harder than a human fingernail, rating about 3.5 on the Mohs scale. It is primarily white in color but can also be light gray, light yellow, or red. Boehmite typically forms through the weathering of rocks in tropical climates.

Boehmite is formed from the same elements as the mineral diaspore. Both minerals contain aluminum, oxygen, and hydrogen. However, the two minerals have different crystal structures. These different structures are due to different temperature and pressure conditions during mineral formation. Two minerals that have different structures but contain the same elements are called dimorphous.

KEEPING FLAMES AT BAY

Boehmite is stable at temperatures of up to 340 degrees Fahrenheit (171°C). This makes it useful for automotive and electronic products that operate at high temperatures. The mineral is used to make catalytic converters, which help control pollution from

Boehmite is named after Johann Böhm, a mineralogist and chemist.

gas engines in motor vehicles. Boehmite is also used as a flame
retardant in printed circuit boards. These are nonconductive
bases on which a network of conductive connections are
placed. The connections allow electricity to flow between
electronic components.

CASSITERITE

Cassiterite is the primary ore of tin. It is a heavy, hard mineral with a Mohs rating of 6 to 7. Pure cassiterite is colorless, but it can be black or brown if impurities are present. If the mineral is found with iron, it can sometimes be red brown or yellow brown in color. Cassiterite typically forms when mineral-rich fluids flow through cracks in rocks. The fluids deposit minerals as they cool. Cassiterite pieces can be carried along by water and deposited in riverbeds or along coastlines.

ROLE IN HUMAN SOCIETY

Cassiterite and tin have played a key role in human societies. Around 5,000 years ago, people began mixing tin with copper to make bronze. They realized that bronze tools and weapons were more durable than those made of other metals. Today, people use tin to coat steel food cans. It is also a popular metal in solder. This material is heated and then used to permanently hold metal parts together. Malaysia, Indonesia, and Bolivia mine most of the world's cassiterite.

CHROMITE

Chromite is the primary ore of chromium. This metallic-black mineral is typically found within rock in masses or veins. Chromite forms when magma cools and solidifies into layers of rock. The mineral can also be found in meteorites, or rocks from space that fall to Earth's surface. Chromite has a Mohs rating of 5.5.

CHROMIUM METAL

Chromium is a hard, gray metal that is commonly added to alloys to boost their strength and make them resistant to corrosion, or rust. Chromium is also used to make knives,

Chromite ranges in color from dark gray to black.

paints, dyes, and stains. Historically, people used chromium to make leather out of animal hides. This process is called tanning. Tanning with chromium is less common in modern times due to the toxic wastes it produces. Today, South Africa is home to most known chromite deposits.

COLUMBITE

Columbite is an important ore of the metal niobium. It is sometimes called niobite. Dense, heavy columbite can be dark gray, black, or brownish black in color. After the mineral is cut or broken, its surfaces may have a blue shine. Columbite has a Mohs rating of 6.

Along with niobium, columbite frequently contains iron and manganese. It is often found alongside another metal, tantalum, in pegmatites. Pegmatites are coarse-grained rocks with large interlocking crystals. Because of columbite's heavy weight, pieces of the mineral that break off can often be found at the bottom of riverbeds and along coastlines.

Niobium is used in medical equipment such as magnetic resonance imaging (MRI) machines.

POWERFUL AND VERSATILE

Niobium is highly resistant to corrosion. It is added to alloys such as stainless steel to create stronger materials for the construction of jets and buildings. Niobium is also a superconductor at temperatures below −443 degrees Fahrenheit (−264°C). Superconductors are materials through which electrical currents can flow with little to no resistance. This superconducting ability allows niobium to be used to create the powerful magnetic fields needed for some medical scanning devices. Niobium is used in eyeglasses too. It allows opticians to create thinner lenses, even for strong prescriptions. Today, Brazil and Canada are the top columbite-producing countries.

Columbite minerals are often opaque and dense. They sometimes have an iridescent luster.

CORUNDUM

Corundum is second only to diamond in hardness, with a Mohs rating of 9. Ruby and sapphire gemstones are both varieties of corundum. Corundum's hardness makes it useful for grinding glass and polishing metals. Pure corundum is colorless. Impurities within the mineral create corundum in shades of gray, white, black, red, or blue.

When corundum is found with other oxide minerals, it forms a popular abrasive material called emery. This is why some nail files are called emery boards. The black emery variety of corundum can erode and crumble into black sand.

ROCK-FORMING MINERALS AND ACCESSORY MINERALS

Minerals are divided into two types: rock-forming minerals and accessory minerals. Rock-forming minerals, such as corundum, make up igneous, sedimentary, or metamorphic rocks. Feldspar, quartz, amphibole, mica, olivine, garnet, calcite, and pyroxene are all rock-forming minerals. Their chemical content reflects Earth's most common elements. Accessory minerals occur in smaller amounts within these rocks. Accessory minerals within a rock can help geologists learn more about the rock's history. Apatite, monazite, zircon, pyrite, titanite, and tourmaline are accessory minerals.

HEAT PLUS PRESSURE

Corundum can be found in multiple rock types. It typically forms under high-temperature and high-pressure conditions. This means it can often be found in rocks that have changed, or metamorphosed, from their original form. Today, India is the world's largest producer of corundum.

Sapphire is a popular gemstone for jewelry. It gets its blue color from iron and titanium impurities within corundum.

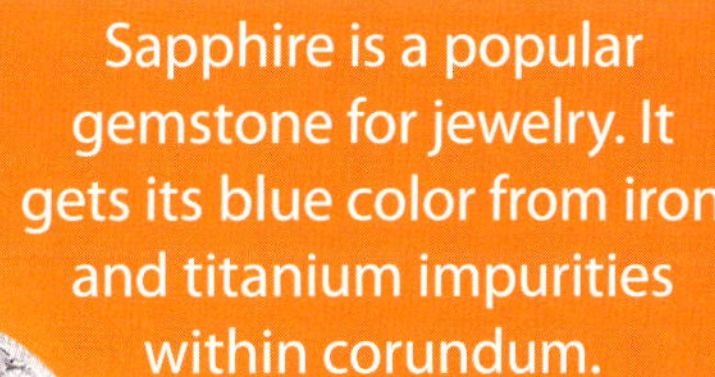

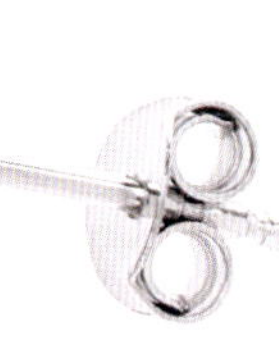

DIASPORE

Diaspore is one of three key minerals in bauxite. The mineral can change color in different light sources. In natural light, diaspore may appear colorless, white, or gray. The mineral may be pink or reddish under light bulbs or candlelight. A stunning deposit of diaspore crystals was found in Turkey in the 1950s. It was discovered during a bauxite mining operation. This discovery, along with diaspore's Mohs rating of 6.5 to 7, spurred interest in the mineral as a gemstone.

A SECONDARY MINERAL

Diaspore is a secondary mineral. Secondary minerals are created when rocks become weathered after their initial formation. Diaspore is often found on the surface of clay and limestone deposits. While some mineral and gem collectors value the mineral, it has limited uses. Diaspore can withstand high temperatures and harsh chemicals. This refractory property makes diaspore a good building material for kilns and furnaces.

Diaspore crystals sometimes form in a V shape.

Some varieties of diaspore
are used as gemstones.
Zultanite, a type of diaspore
found in Turkey, is valued for
its color-changing abilities.

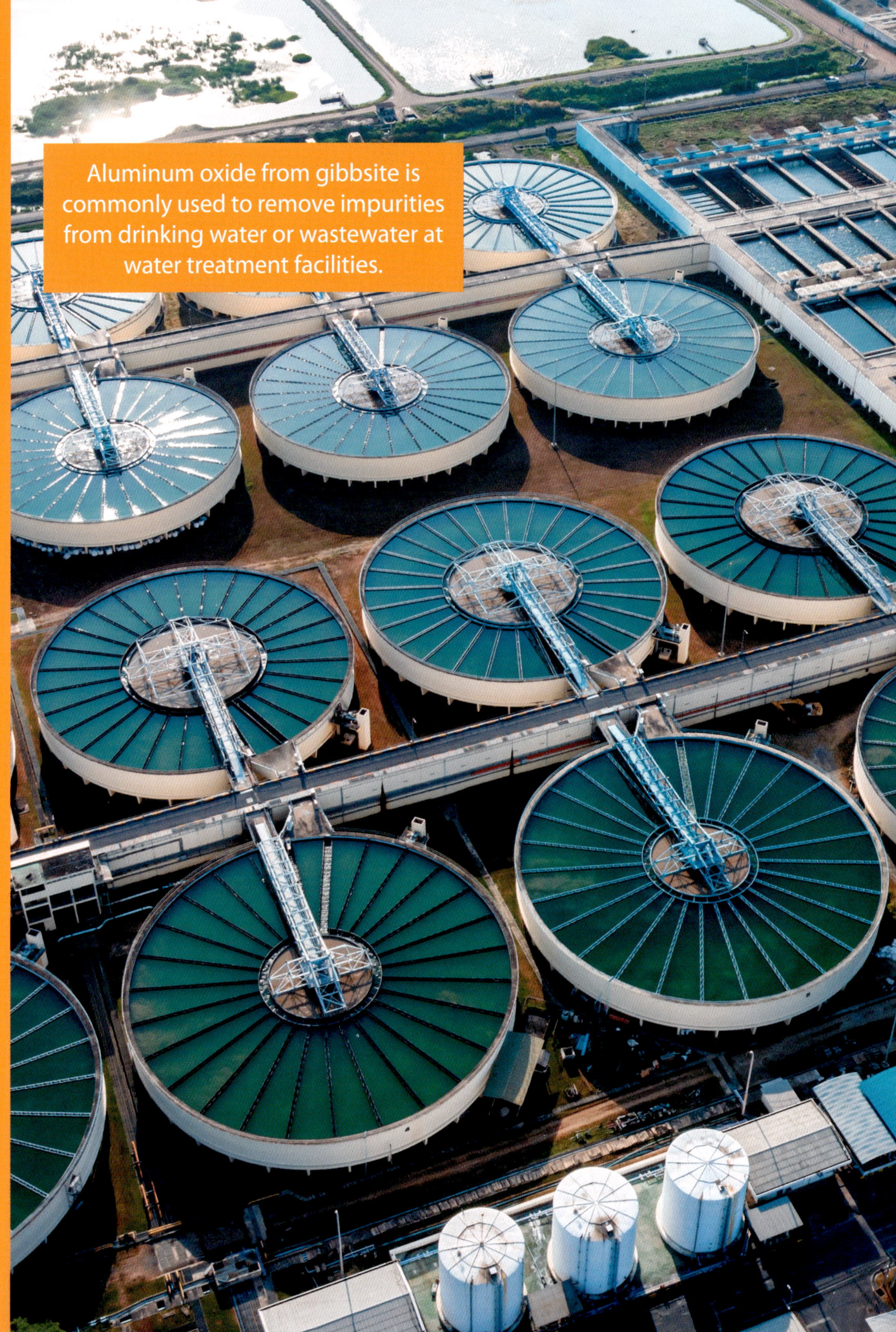
Aluminum oxide from gibbsite is commonly used to remove impurities from drinking water or wastewater at water treatment facilities.

GIBBSITE

Gibbsite is one of three key minerals in bauxite. It comes in a range of colors. Gibbsite can be white, gray, or colorless. It can also be green, yellow, and reddish brown. It is a soft, secondary mineral that forms on top of other minerals through the process of weathering. Some gibbsite deposits are found on top of boehmite, which is another component of bauxite.

FROM ALUMINUM TO WATER TREATMENT

Geologists study gibbsite deposits to learn more about Earth's structure. The mineral forms under intense weathering conditions in warm, wet climates. The presence of gibbsite is a clue that an area was once warm and wet, regardless of its current environment. Today, the primary use of gibbsite is in aluminum refining. Gibbsite also can be used in water treatment facilities to help trap impurities. Australia, Guinea, and China are the world's leading producers of gibbsite.

HEMATITE

Hematite is a hard, heavy, and relatively common mineral. It ranges from black to silver gray in color. Hematite is the source of about 90 percent of the iron produced in the United States. The mineral is known for the streak of reddish brown that it leaves behind when scraped against another surface. Even black hematite samples streak and turn red when finely ground. Rust is a form of hematite.

Hematite is found in many rocks around the world. It forms in sedimentary deposits when iron precipitates from, or comes out of, iron-rich water. Hematite can also be created when mineral-rich water cools as it leaves hydrothermal openings. It can form when other minerals are

Minerals such as hematite can be identified by the powdery streak they leave behind. A streak test can be done using an unglazed porcelain tile, or streak plate.

exposed to intense heat or pressure too. Hematite has even been found in rocks on Mars.

FORGING IRON AND STEEL

Hematite plays a role in the steel industry. Iron from hematite is heated up with various elements to create molten iron. This iron is mixed with other metals to create steel. Hematite is also used as a pigment in cosmetics and paints. It serves as a polishing material too.

ILMENITE

Ilmenite is an important ore of the metal titanium. This shiny mineral can be dark black, gray, or brown. Ilmenite is commonly found with hematite. It can be found in large masses, within veins in rocks, and within black sands. The mineral was named after Russia's Ilmen Mountains, where it was first discovered. Scientists later discovered ilmenite in rocks that US astronauts collected on the Moon. Ilmenite has a Mohs rating of 5 to 6.

Today, ilmenite is the source of about 82 percent of the world's titanium.

FOR THE BRIGHTEST WHITES

Titanium metal extracted from ilmenite is exceptionally strong and lightweight. It is the preferred material for human joint replacements. Titanium is resistant to corrosion from bodily fluids. Most titanium is used to make titanium dioxide. This produces the bright white color of paper, paint, and even toothpaste. China is the world's leading producer of ilmenite, followed by Mozambique.

LIMONITE

Limonite is an iron-rich mixture of minerals that forms on top of other minerals. This formation happens in the presence of water and oxygen. Limonite typically forms on rocks, clay, and gravel in cool, wet environments. These include marshes, swamps, and areas with soil. Ranking 4 to 5.5 on the Mohs scale, limonite is a semisoft mineral that often appears dull yellow, brown, or reddish brown in color.

CAPTURING IMPURITIES

Limonite is sometimes known as bog iron. Limonite, hematite, and magnetite are the primary ores of iron. Limonite is also used in wastewater treatment processes to remove impurities such as arsenic and lead. Substances that collect and hold other substances in this way are called adsorbents. For centuries, artists have also used limonite as a pigment. The mineral is in yellow, brown, and earth-tone pigments. Limonite deposits can be found around the world.

Limonite has long been used to create ocher pigments. Aboriginal peoples in Australia used these pigments to create rock art.

Limonite minerals can take many forms, but they do not form into crystals.

MAGNETITE

Magnetite is nature's most magnetic mineral. It is one of three key iron ores, along with hematite and limonite. Magnetite is common in most igneous and metamorphic rocks. The mineral is harder than glass. It is known for its metallic-black color and for its magnetic properties. It leaves a black streak behind when rubbed across hard surfaces.

People in ancient China used a type of magnetite called lodestone to create compasses. Lodestone was fashioned into a spoon shape and placed on a flat surface.

Magnetite has played a pivotal role in society. Early humans learned to magnetize pieces of iron by striking them with magnetite. This led to the invention of the compass, an important navigation tool used in trade, exploration, and warfare. The iron from magnetite also affected the development of modern tools, factories, and vehicles.

NATURAL COMPASS FOR EARTH'S HISTORY

Today, magnetite is found all around the world. The mineral offers clues about Earth's history. Magnetite within igneous and metamorphic rocks aligns with Earth's magnetic field at the time the rock forms. This position stays the same even as Earth's magnetic field changes. This creates a historical record of the planet's magnetic field that geologists can study.

DID YOU KNOW?

In the past, magnetite's magnetic properties meant that ships carrying it could not rely on compasses to determine a heading, or direction. Today, Global Positioning System (GPS) technology allows people to navigate without magnets.

PEROVSKITE

Perovskite is an ore of titanium that often contains REEs. The mineral can be black, grayish black, or brownish black. It can even include red and yellow hues if iron or copper are present. Perovskite is a medium-hard metal with a Mohs rating of 5.5. The mineral was first identified in Russia. It has since been found in igneous rocks in Italy, Switzerland, and the US state of Arkansas.

SUPERCONDUCTING WONDER

Perovskite is highly valued for its ability to carry electrical currents. It is used in

Perovskite sometimes has cube-shaped crystals.

electronics and solar panels. Perovskite can absorb energy from the Sun and convert it into electricity more efficiently than many other materials can. Some forms of perovskite are superconducting. This means they can efficiently conduct electricity at very low temperatures.

In 2021, a Polish company launched a new type of solar panel sheet made with perovskite film.

RUTILE

Rutile is an ore of titanium. It is the most common source of titanium dioxide. Rutile occurs in a variety of colors, including reddish brown, black, and yellow. The mineral produces a white streak when scraped against hard surfaces. Its beautiful crystals and hardness make rutile popular among collectors. The mineral is sometimes used as a gemstone.

A USEFUL TOOL

Rutile can be found in igneous, metamorphic, and sedimentary rocks. It often occurs alongside other ore deposits. Roughly 95 percent of titanium from rutile is used as a pigment in paint, plastics, and ink. The mineral is also used as a coating for welding tools. Rutile has one of the highest refractive indexes

Rutile can take many different forms and have different crystal patterns.

in nature. This means light passing through rutile bends more than it does in most other substances. This makes rutile an excellent material for optical products such as camera lenses and microscopes. Australia is the world's largest producer of rutile, followed by South Africa and Sierra Leone.

SAMARSKITE

Samarskite is a heavy, radioactive mineral. It is a source of the rare earth metal samarium. Samarskite deposits frequently include the radioactive elements uranium and thorium. The mineral features a black interior under a yellow-brown surface. It is a medium-hard mineral with a Mohs rating of 5 to 6.

Samarskite is named after Colonel Vasili Samarsky-Bykhovets, a Russian mining engineer.

RADIOACTIVE MINERALS

Some minerals emit a form of energy called radiation. Minerals that contain the elements uranium, thorium, and potassium are radioactive. Radioactive materials can be useful, but they must be handled carefully. Exposure to too much radiation can harm living tissues. Rocks with radioactive components can also help geologists learn about Earth's history. Radioactive materials naturally decay over time at a known rate. Geologists can measure this decay to determine a rock's age.

KEY TO STRONGER MAGNETS

Samarium is often combined with cobalt. This produces strong, permanent magnets that are used in motors and electronics. Samarium's magnetic strength at high temperatures allows companies to make very small speakers, such as those in headphones. Samarium can also absorb some types of radiation. This led to its use in infrared-absorbing glass and nuclear reactors. People in the entertainment industry use samarium for special lights in projectors and studios.

Samarskite deposits can be found worldwide. The mineral is often found in pegmatites. These igneous rocks include large interlocking crystals and can be a source of REEs. Leading producers of samarskite include China, Russia, and Malaysia.

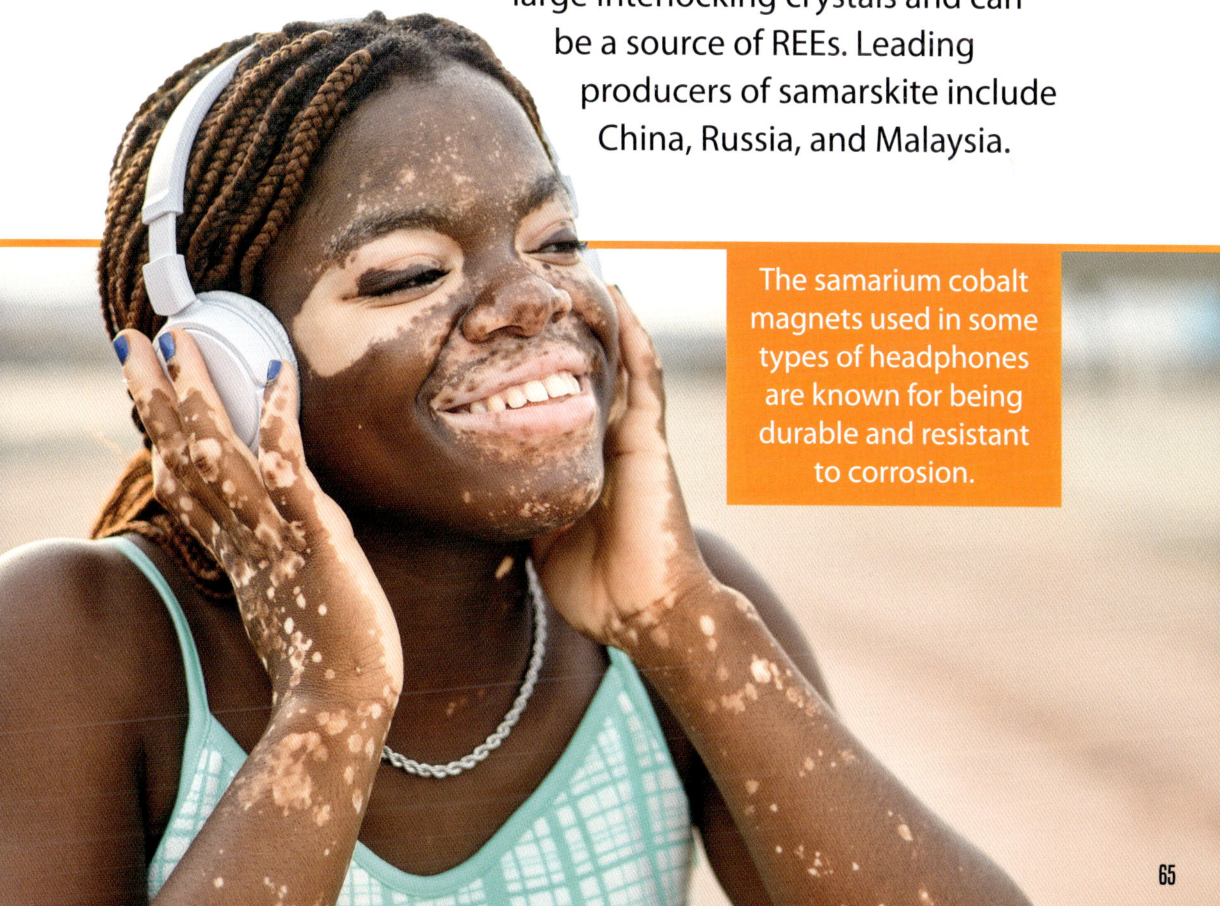

The samarium cobalt magnets used in some types of headphones are known for being durable and resistant to corrosion.

SPINEL

Spinel is an uncommon mineral that is famous for its range of colors. Pure spinel is a colorless combination of aluminum and magnesium. But spinel is more commonly found in shades of red, pink, purple, blue, and sometimes black. Its colors depend on which other elements are included in it. Blue spinel crystals get their color from cobalt, while red spinel crystals get their color from chromium. Red spinel gems are sometimes mistaken for rubies. Due to its Mohs rating of 7.5 to 8 and its variety of colors, spinel is a popular gemstone.

NATURAL HEAT RESISTANCE

Spinel forms under high pressures and high temperatures. It is used to create heat-resistant parts for jets, rockets, and electronics. The mineral's strength also makes it a good material for cutting, grinding, and shaping other materials. Most spinel is found in Southeast Asia and Africa. Myanmar and Sri Lanka are leading producers of the mineral.

One famous spinel gem is the Black Prince's Ruby, which is on the Imperial State Crown of England. King Charles wore this crown during his 2023 coronation.
Black Prince's Ruby

TANTALITE

Tantalite is a primary source of tantalum, an REE. It also can include iron or manganese. Tantalite can have a metallic sheen and may be opaque or slightly transparent. It comes in dark to medium tones of gray, red, and brown. The tough mineral is about as hard as a steel nail.

TAKING ON TOUGH JOBS

Tantalum is a strong, shiny metal that is resistant to corrosion. It is often used in cell phones, computers, and airplanes. Tantalum can be applied in a thin layer on electrical components. This helps store energy and keep electrical currents in place. When combined with graphite, tantalum

Tantalite is a moderately hard mineral, with a Mohs rating of 6 to 6.5.

creates some of the world's toughest cutting tools. The mineral is also used in artificial joints and other implants. Tantalum does not create problems within human bodies, so bodies do not try to reject it.

Tantalite can be found in many regions within igneous rocks such as granite. It can also be found in places where rock pieces have been deposited by running water. The Democratic Republic of the Congo, Rwanda, and Brazil lead the world in tantalite mining.

Tantalum is used to make electrolytic capacitors in smartphones. These parts help store energy in the device.

Uraninite is sometimes called pitchblende.

URANINITE

Uraninite is the most common source of the radioactive element uranium. The moderately hard uraninite is one of the densest minerals. It is shiny and often comes in shades of black or brownish black. Uraninite can be found worldwide in igneous rocks. The mineral also can be found in the cracks of rock formations. Kazakhstan, Canada, and Australia are leaders in uranium mining. Due to uraninite's radioactive properties, it must be mined and collected carefully.

DISCOVERING RADIOACTIVITY

Uranium is used as fuel in nuclear power plants and nuclear weapons. Uranium compounds can be used as coloring for glass and ceramics too. Uraninite helped French physicist Henri Becquerel discover radioactivity in 1896. Becquerel placed a uraninite sample on photographic paper in a dark, closed drawer. He was surprised to see an image when he later developed the paper. Normally, sunlight was needed to create an image on photographic paper. Becquerel realized that something besides the Sun was producing the image. His discovery helped scientists learn more about different kinds of radiation, or energy that travels in a combination of waves and particles.

Henri Becquerel
was awarded the
1903 Nobel Prize
in Physics for his
studies of uranium
and radioactivity.

The name *apatite* comes from a Greek word meaning "to deceive." This is because the mineral looks similar to many other types of minerals.

APATITE

The mineral apatite is the primary source of the plant nutrient phosphorus. Apatite contains calcium phosphate. Human and animal bones and teeth also contain calcium phosphate, along with several other substances. In mineral form, apatite is usually found in transparent lumps, masses, or crystals. It comes in a wide range of colors and is slightly softer than glass.

Apatite is commonly found in rocks formed by heat and pressure. It can be found in calcium-rich and phosphorus-rich sedimentary rocks too. Apatite deposits are found around the world. Most of these deposits are mined for phosphate. China and Morocco lead the world in the production of apatite for phosphate.

KEY FOR AGRICULTURE

Most apatite is used to make phosphate fertilizer for agricultural purposes. Phosphate contains the element phosphorus. Phosphorus helps plants turn energy from the Sun into things they need to grow, such as sugar and oxygen. This process is called photosynthesis. Apatite can also be used to make dental implants and bone replacements. Apatite is a source of phosphoric acid too. This is used to preserve foods and give beverages a tangy taste.

Apatite-based phosphate fertilizers are often processed into small granules.

MONAZITE

Monazite is the primary source of the radioactive element thorium. It is also a source of the REEs cerium, lanthanum, and yttrium. Monazite can be found in the form of grains within igneous rocks. Monazite grains found apart from their host rocks can form monazite sands. These are richer in REEs than other sands. Monazite is about as hard as glass. Its brown deposits can include tints of red, yellow, orange, and pink.

India, South Africa, and Madagascar are all home to monazite sand deposits. Cerium from monazite sands is the most abundant of the REEs. People use cerium, lanthanum, and neodymium to make heat-resistant lighting for film projectors

Monazite sand is typically found in placer deposits. These are places where mineral sands build up over time due to natural forces such as weathering.

and studio lights. These materials also can be used to make lighters and heat-resistant glass.

LIGHT WITHOUT LIGHT BULBS

Thorium has many uses due to its high melting point of 1,468 degrees Fahrenheit (798°C). It burns brightly when heated and exposed to oxygen. This allows it to generate incandescent light, or light created by heat, without an electric light bulb. Thorium is used to make camera lenses too. Light refracts, or bends, when it goes through things such as glass or water. Thorium reduces how much the light bends as it goes through a camera lens. This helps keep the light in the ideal position as it goes into the camera.

TORBERNITE

Torbernite is a secondary mineral associated with the uranium-bearing mineral uraninite. Most torbernite forms when oxygen-rich water pulls uranium from uranium ores. It then carries the uranium to places where it can interact with copper and other chemicals. This creates the glassy, bright green crystals of torbernite.

A BEAUTIFUL INDICATOR MINERAL

Because torbernite forms from uranium ores, it can be used to identify possible uranium deposits. The stunning mineral can create high-quality crystals. However, torbernite's radioactivity means that it requires special handling. The mineral is used mostly for radiation research and mining education. Torbernite is frequently found in the Democratic Republic of the Congo and in Cornwall, England.

In 1885, torbernite was discovered at the South Terras Mine in Cornwall, England.

Torbernite crystals can form in many different patterns, including clusters and cubes.

VANADINITE

Vanadinite, which comes in shades of bright red, red orange, or brown, is a secondary mineral of lead deposits. The mineral is also a key ore of the metal vanadium. It forms in places where lead deposits are close enough to Earth's surface to react with oxygen and with vanadium-rich fluids. Vanadinite is a relatively soft mineral, with a Mohs rating of 3 to 4. Vanadinite crystals are popular with mineral collectors. They are most often found in dry regions. Morocco, Mexico, and the southwestern United States are home to major vanadinite deposits.

Vanadinite often forms in hexagonal crystal clusters.

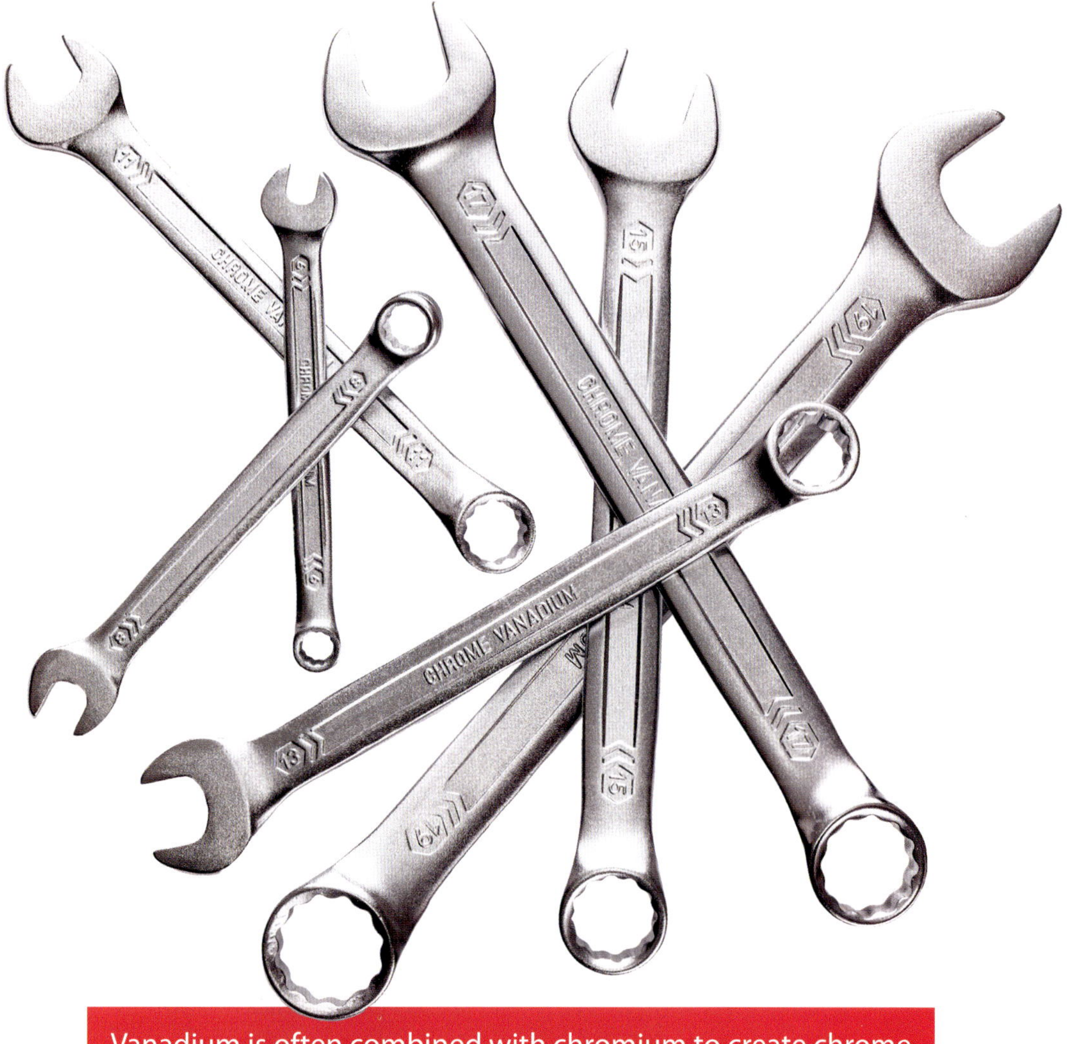

Vanadium is often combined with chromium to create chrome vanadium steel, which is commonly used for hand tools.

A FLEXIBLE METAL

Vanadium is a soft, silver-white metal that can be stretched into thin wires or reshaped without becoming weak or brittle. It is commonly added to steel and cast iron to add strength and durability. Tools, airplanes, machinery, and cars can all benefit from steel blends that include vanadium. China, Russia, and South Africa are major exporters of vanadium for industrial use.

ALLANITE

Allanite is the name for a group of silicate minerals known for their complexity and widespread occurrence. Allanite deposits can contain the REEs cerium, lanthanum, and yttrium. They can contain iron and aluminum too. Allanite minerals have shiny black or brownish-black crystals of varying sizes. These crystals are often nestled within parent rocks such as granite. Allanite minerals have a Mohs rating of 5.5 to 6.5. They are frequently discovered alongside the minerals biotite and garnet.

Geologists study allanite deposits to learn more about Earth's history and composition. The minerals formed during periods of extreme heat, intense pressure, and hot magma flows. They were also made when superheated water in Earth's crust

Allanite minerals often feature slender, rod-shaped crystals.

Allanite was first discovered in 1810. It is named after Scottish mineralogist Thomas Allan.

interacted with existing rock structures. Allanite deposits are clues that geologic processes such as extreme heat, pressure, or hydrothermal activity occurred in a certain area. These clues can lead to the discovery of other minerals that formed through similar geologic processes.

MANY USES

Allanite's diverse elements have many uses. Neodymium from allanite deposits can be used to create powerful magnets. Europium and terbium from allanite minerals can be used to make lights and screens that shine without the need for heat. Many important industries, including renewable energy and medical imaging, use the REEs contained in allanite deposits.

AMPHIBOLE

Amphibole minerals are commonly found in rocks that formed far below Earth's surface. These black, dark green, or dark brown minerals may have a metallic sheen. They are harder than glass, rating 5 to 6 on the Mohs scale.

Nephrite, a green amphibole mineral, is similar to jade. It has been used to make jewelry and statues for centuries. Amphibole minerals provided the first source of asbestos. Asbestos is the name for a group of heat-resistant mineral fibers. In ancient Rome, people wove asbestos fibers into body coverings before dead bodies were cremated. The asbestos fibers kept the body coverings intact even as the bodies themselves burned. This made it easier to collect the ashes of the dead after cremation. Later, asbestos was used in many building materials to make them resistant to fire.

Asbestos was once widely used in buildings' insulation, walls, siding, and more. Today, some older homes still contain asbestos.

POPULAR BUILDING MATERIALS

Amphiboles are durable minerals that can be polished to a high sheen. This makes them popular for paving and decoration. Roads and railbed projects may use crushed, locally sourced amphiboles due to their widespread availability.

DID YOU KNOW?

Today, asbestos is no longer a preferred fire-resistant material. If a person inhales asbestos fibers, the fibers can become trapped in the person's lungs. This increases the risk of lung cancer.

Nephrite amphibole has long been valued by the Māori people of New Zealand. They use the mineral to create carvings and jewelry.

ANDALUSITE

Andalusite minerals formed deep within Earth under intense heat and pressure. This makes them highly durable and heat resistant. Andalusite deposits appear in shades of brown mixed with green, orange, yellow, and red. Other variations have pink, gray, and white hues. Some andalusite minerals feature a unique checkerboard pattern that can be seen when the mineral is cut. Andalusites are hard minerals with a Mohs rating of up to 7.5.

Ceramic manufacturers use andalusite minerals to make strong products that are resistant to extreme temperatures. Historically, these minerals were added to the porcelain insulators in spark plugs because they could withstand high temperatures without breaking. Makers of industrial kilns and furnaces also use andalusite minerals in the linings of high-temperature equipment.

METAMORPHISM INDICATOR

Geologists study andalusite deposits to learn about Earth's history. If andalusite minerals are present in an area, it means that the area once experienced high temperatures and intense pressure. These factors can change the chemistry, texture, and composition of rocks. This process is called metamorphism. South Africa, France, and Peru are the world's top andalusite-producing nations.

Industrial kilns and furnaces are often lined with andalusite bricks. The mineral is also used to make the supports and shelves that go inside kilns and furnaces.

Bertrandite was
discovered in
France in 1883.

BERTRANDITE

Bertrandite is second only to beryl as an ore of beryllium metal. It is often colorless or pale yellow, and it has a Mohs rating of 6 to 7. In some deposits, bertrandite replaces beryl while maintaining the same overall shape. A mineral that replaces another while retaining the same shape is called a pseudomorph. Pseudomorphs can form when underground fluids leach some elements out of a mineral and replace them with other elements.

A SURPRISING GEMSTONE

Some forms of bertrandite include elements that give the mineral purple, pink, and blue colors. People call this gemstone Tiffany stone. Colorless forms of bertrandite are often used for beryllium ore processing. Utah's Spor Mountain is one of the world's leading producers of beryllium from bertrandite. Beryllium from Spor Mountain is used in metal alloys. It is also used in the nuclear energy and aerospace industries.

Tiffany stone is sometimes called ice cream stone because of its vibrant swirls of color.

BERYL

Beryl is a prized gemstone and the primary source of the metal beryllium. Beryl's many colors result in multiple gemstones. Green emeralds, pink morganites, and blue-green aquamarines are all varieties of beryl. The mineral is a hard gemstone, with a Mohs rating of 7.5 to 8.

HIGH-TECH METAL

Beryllium is a lightweight, silvery metal. It has a high strength-to-weight ratio. This means it can make alloys stronger without adding a lot of extra weight to them. It is also somewhat elastic. Adding beryllium to metal alloys for products such as springs or gears gives those items the ability to flex without breaking. Beryllium alloys are used in electronics, cars, computers, and even spacecraft. An alloy of

Emeralds are among the most popular and valuable beryl gemstones.

beryllium and copper is used in gasoline pumps because the mixture does not spark from static electricity.

The United States produces most of the world's beryllium. Colombia, Brazil, and Madagascar are key producers of gem-quality beryl. Beryl forms slowly in environments that are rich in beryllium, aluminum, and silicon and that experience relatively high pressure. Beryl deposits can be found worldwide. They tend to occur within coarse-grained rocks and rock veins. These veins are formed by mineral-rich fluids flowing through cracks.

BIOTITE

Biotite is the most common mineral within a group of flaky minerals called mica. It can be brown, black, or sometimes green. Biotite and its close relative phlogopite have layered crystal structures. Both minerals are about as hard as a human fingernail. They can be easily peeled into thin, semitransparent sheets. Biotite is a rock-forming mineral. It is abundant in rocks produced under high temperatures, such as granite.

A VERSATILE MINERAL

Traditionally, biotite sheets have been used as insulation in heating systems. The mineral is also used as a filler in paints and rubber products. Biotite can be used in oil and gas exploration as a drilling mud. Drilling muds are gel-like fluids that are

Biotite is a soft mineral, rating just 2.5 to 3 on the Mohs scale.

Drilling mud containing biotite is often stored in large tanks.

pumped into wells, or holes in the ground, as they are drilled in the search for oil and gas resources. Drilling muds help hold the well space open by pushing against its sides. They help prevent drill bits from overheating. They also help move rock shavings and other debris away from the drilling area. Biotite can teach geologists about mineral properties too. Studying biotite's chemical composition can help geologists determine how old rocks and minerals are. It can also help them learn about the conditions under which minerals formed.

CERITE

Cerite is a source of the metallic REE cerium. It can often be found near other cerium-containing minerals such as bastnäsite or allanite. The reddish-brown mineral rates 5.5 on the Mohs scale. The term *cerite* can also refer to a group of minerals. Aside from cerium, these minerals can contain calcium, lanthanum, and magnesium.

MANY USES

Cerium is used in many industries. It is a common component in catalytic converters in motor vehicles. In the glass industry, cerium is used for polishing. Adding cerium to metal alloys can improve their strength and ability to resist rust. Combining cerium with lanthanum, neodymium, iron, and other metallic REEs creates misch metal. Misch metal is used in lighters. It is also used to remove unwanted oxygen from metal mixtures. Cerite concentrations can be found in Sweden, Russia, Canada, and the United States.

Cerite minerals have been found at Sweden's Bastnäs Mine.

Cerium is the main component of misch metal. This metal acts as the flint in lighters, helping to spark flames.

CLAYS

Clays are fine-grained minerals that are abundant worldwide. Different kinds of clays have different contents. Clays are made mostly of aluminum and silicon, but there can be other elements and impurities within them. Clays come from rocks that break down into tiny particles over thousands of years. Volcanic ash can become clay too. Most clays are mined from open pits.

Clays tend to be light in color. They can trap and hold liquids. They can be shaped when mixed with water. Clays can catch and hold other substances too. They stick to things like a covering. These abilities make clays very useful.

MULTIPURPOSE MINERALS

Clays are most commonly used for making bricks, pottery, and ceramics. The oldest known pottery was made around 20,000 years ago. Throughout history, people also used clays for medicinal purposes. Some were used to cover wounds. Modern clays help pet litter

Utah's Bentonite Hills are made of bentonite clay, which contains the clay mineral montmorillonite.

absorb liquids. They keep oil drills from overheating. Clay minerals can also help remove pollutants from contaminated soils and wastewater. Clays can even slow the release of nutrients from fertilizer to better support plant growth.

A LIFETIME OF MINERALS

The average American is estimated to use more than 3 million pounds (1.4 million kg) of minerals, metals, and fuels in his or her lifetime. This includes more than 197,000 pounds (89,358 kg) of coal and 11,703 pounds (5,308 kg) of clay. The average American also will use 1.35 million pounds (612,350 kg) of stone, sand, and gravel; 930 pounds (422 kg) of bauxite; and more than 28,000 pounds (12,701 kg) of salt. He or she will use 930 pounds (422 kg) of copper, 853 pounds (387 kg) of lead, and 1.7 pounds (0.77 kg) of lithium.

DIOPSIDE

Diopside is a medium-hard mineral that rates 5 to 6 on the Mohs scale. It is known for its green color. But the mineral also can have hues of gray, yellow, blue, purple, and white. Diopside shares a crystal structure with the mineral hedenbergite. Sometimes both minerals are found in the same sample. Two minerals that share a structure but are made of different elements are called a series.

Geologists study diopside to better understand how rocks form. Diopside is commonly found in a type of rock called skarn. Skarn forms when igneous rock–forming materials such as magma meet cooler sedimentary rock materials.

This reaction releases mineral-rich fluids from the igneous material as it cools. The fluids dissolve, replacing the existing minerals with new ones. This process is called metasomatism.

DIAMOND INDICATOR

Some high-quality diopside specimens can be gemstones. But diopside is most valuable as an indicator mineral. Diopside's bright green color makes it easy to find. It is frequently found alongside rocks that are known for bearing diamonds.

Diamonds are commonly found in a type of rock called kimberlite, *pictured*. Diopside is often located near kimberlite deposits.

FELDSPAR

Feldspar is a group of rock-forming minerals. This group makes up more than half of Earth's crust. Feldspar is typically white, pink, gray, or brown. The mineral is roughly as hard as a steel nail. It is found in igneous, metamorphic, and sedimentary rocks. It is found in soils and clays too.

MAKING THINGS STRONGER

Many common household products depend on feldspar. The mineral makes it easier and less expensive to make glass bottles and windowpanes. Adding feldspar to glass mixtures helps the mixtures melt at lower temperatures. This saves money by using less energy. Feldspar also makes glass easier to shape by making molten glass less thick and slow moving. Feldspar can create stronger, more durable ceramic tiles, plates, and cups. It is also used as a filler in paints, insulation, and roadbeds. This creates smoother mixtures with less

All feldspars contain aluminum, oxygen, and silicon.

Feldspar is used as a flux in glass production. This makes glass used for windowpanes and other items more durable.

space between granular components.

Feldspar deposits occur around the globe. The mineral is commonly found on Earth's surface. North Carolina, Virginia, and California are the top feldspar producers in the United States.

DID YOU KNOW?

Some minerals found on Earth have also been found in rocks on the Moon and Mars. These extraterrestrial rocks experience less chemical weathering than rocks on Earth do. Extraterrestrial rocks frequently contain plagioclase feldspar and pyroxene. Both these minerals are easily changed by chemical weathering.

GADOLINITE

Gadolinite is prized for its rare earth metals, including gadolinium. The mineral is dark black, brown, or greenish black. It ranks 6.5 to 7 on the Mohs scale. Gadolinite was first discovered in Ytterby, Sweden, in 1787. Mining operations around Ytterby also produced the first known REE metals. Several rare earth metals, including yttrium, ytterbium, terbium, and erbium, are named after Ytterby.

Gadolinium is a flexible, silvery metal that can do unusual things at different temperatures. Cold gadolinium can be more magnetic than iron. Placing gadolinium in a magnetic field warms it up. Removing it from that field cools the metal back down. Gadolinium is a superconducting material. This means it can conduct electricity with little to no resistance when it's very cold. Doctors sometimes inject gadolinium into patients before magnetic resonance imaging (MRI) testing. This helps them clearly see inside the patient's body. Gadolinium is also used to make microwave ovens, television sets, and computer chips.

HARD TO FIND

The 17 rare earth metals are relatively abundant in Earth's crust. However, they tend to be found in very small amounts. Minerals containing REEs may also include some radioactive elements. Gadolinite isn't usually mined on its own. Instead, it's typically mined alongside other REE-containing minerals.

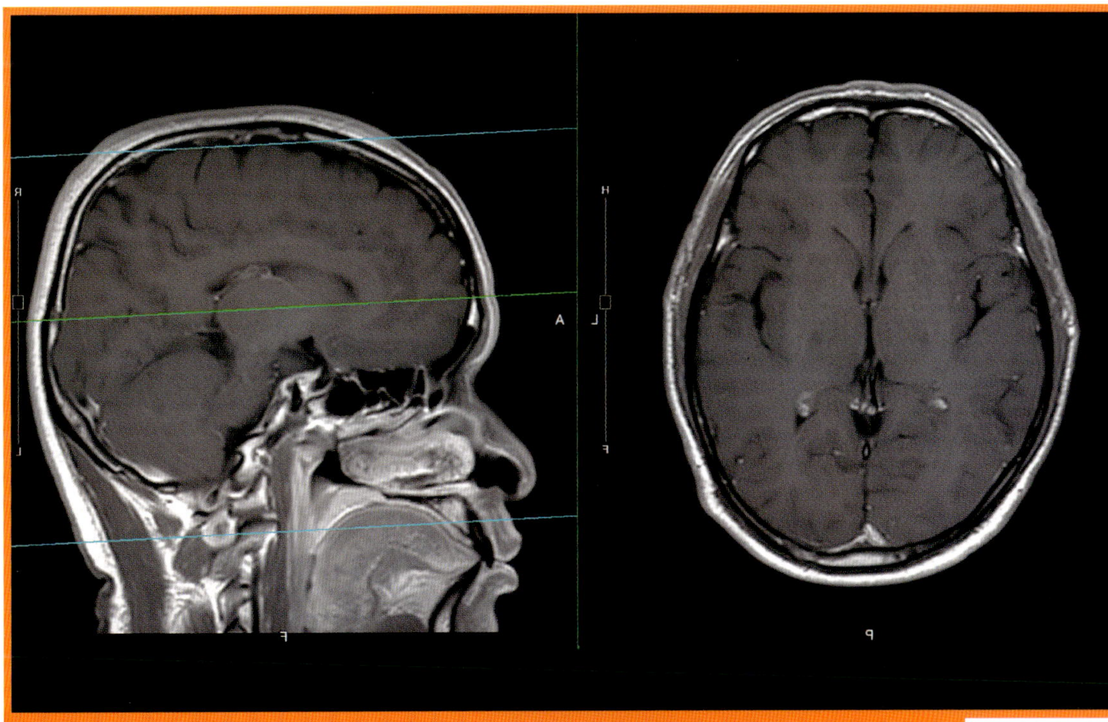

The gadolinium-based liquids that doctors use for MRI testing are known as MRI contrast agents. These enhance the clarity of MRI images.

GARNET

Garnets are a group of minerals that feature similar structures in a variety of colors. Most garnets are red. But the minerals can be found in nearly every color except blue. The small, rounded crystals are found in all major rock types. They are about as hard as steel nails. Because of their unique shape and color, garnets have been described as looking like pomegranate seeds trapped inside rock.

A PRIZED STONE

Garnets have long been prized as gemstones. People in ancient Egypt valued the minerals. Garnets' widespread availability and durability have made the mineral a popular abrasive. Many modern sandpapers are made with garnets. Garnet sand is used in sandblasting since it generates less dust than quartz-based sand. Sandblasting uses compressed

Garnet has a Mohs rating of 6.5 to 7.5, making it a popular gemstone for jewelry.

air to spray sand particles at objects, which removes paint or other finishes. Garnets are also used to polish glass lenses and materials for electronic components.

Garnet is found worldwide in places that once experienced intense heat and pressure. Bright red garnets are an indicator of such metamorphic conditions. Australia and China lead the world in industrial garnet production.

HEMIMORPHITE

Hemimorphite is an ore of the metal zinc. The mineral appears in traditional crystal forms but also in globular forms that look like clusters of grapes. Hemimorphite crystals vary in color. They can be white, yellow, green, gray, or blue. The mineral ranks 4.5 to 5 on the Mohs scale.

Zinc is a bluish-white metal and a common element in Earth's crust. It is often used as a protective covering, or plate. Zinc plating is applied on top of metals that tend to rust. This process is called galvanizing. Zinc is also used to produce compounds used in paints, rubber, chemicals, and agricultural products.

SECONDARY ZINC SOURCE

Hemimorphite forms as a secondary mineral when other zinc-containing ores undergo the process of weathering. Sometimes mineral-rich fluids cool and create hemimorphite in the crevices of existing rocks. Hemimorphite is found worldwide. China, Australia, and Peru are major producers of zinc from hemimorphite and other zinc ores.

Some hemimorphite minerals have bright blue or green colors. Many people collect these colorful minerals.

WEATHERING

Weathering refers to processes that break down rocks over time. This can happen due to water, weather, and chemicals such as acids or salts. Sometimes weathering leaves minerals intact. Other times, it changes their composition. Weathering is one of the ways in which secondary minerals form. Secondary minerals also can form when hot, mineral-rich hydrothermal fluids change an existing mineral's chemical composition.

During the galvanizing process, metal is usually dipped in a bath of liquid zinc to get its protective coating.

ILLITE

Illite is a type of clay mineral. Unlike many clays, illite does not swell much when it gets wet. This fine-grained, grayish-white mineral is often found in sedimentary rock that formed underwater. Illite can be found in soils and some metamorphic rocks too. The mineral is smooth to the touch and very soft.

A HELPFUL ADDITIVE

Illite is often added to paint to help make it resistant to fading. It is also used to remove impurities during wastewater treatment. Farmers may use illite to remove contaminants from soil. The mineral is often added to paper to make it stronger and brighter. Oil and gas producers also use illite in drilling muds because it keeps the mud flowing even as temperatures increase.

Illite forms as a secondary mineral from muscovite and feldspar. This happens due to weathering and reactions with mineral-rich fluids. The mineral is found around the world. China, the United States, Ukraine, and Germany are leaders in industrial illite production.

KAOLINITE

Kaolinite is a common clay mineral formed by the weathering of feldspar-rich rocks. It is usually white, but impurities can add red, blue, or brown tints to the mineral. Soft and versatile, kaolinite is roughly as hard as a human fingernail. It is typically collected from naturally occurring clay beds.

OLD MINERAL

Humans have been using kaolinite for pottery since the 1200s. Today, industries use kaolinite to create whiter, glossier paper. Kaolinite may account for up to one-third of the weight of some magazines. People continue to use the mineral to make ceramics and porcelain. Kaolinite also plays a role in personal

Rocks that contain kaolinite are called kaolin.

care products, including toothpaste and makeup, and spa treatments. For centuries, the mineral has been used to treat skin conditions such as poison ivy or diaper rash.

Kaolinite is found worldwide. It is commonly found in areas where rocks eroded in hot, humid climates. China leads the world in kaolinite production, followed by the United States.

DID YOU KNOW?

Scientists study how clay can help kill antibiotic-resistant bacteria. Researchers have found that clays rich in iron and aluminum can kill bacteria cells. The clays poison the bacteria with iron. Blue and green clays are most effective for this purpose.

KYANITE

Kyanite is a mineral created under heat and pressure. These factors cause aluminum and silica in parent rocks to recrystallize. Kyanite is usually blue in color but can also be green, gray, or colorless. The mineral's hardness level varies depending on the direction in which it is cut. When kyanite is crosscut, it has a Mohs rating of 6.5 to 7. But when it is cut lengthwise, the mineral has a rating of 4.5 to 5.

Kyanite is found in mountain ranges and other areas where the plates that make up Earth's crust shifted, thrusting formerly buried landscapes to the surface. The mineral is highly refractory, or heat resistant. This makes it an ideal material for kilns and furnaces. Adding kyanite to materials such as glass or porcelain can make them less likely to break when exposed to sudden, extreme temperature changes.

A RARE BEAUTY

Kyanite is a relatively rare mineral. It is found most frequently in the Appalachian Mountains in the United States. It is also common in Asia's Himalayan mountain range and the European Alps. South Africa, the United States, France, and India are leading producers of kyanite.

The name *kyanite* comes from the Greek word *kyanos*, which means "deep blue."

The world's largest kyanite mine is located in Virginia. It is in the Piedmont region at the base of the Appalachian Mountains.

Lepidolite's purple and pink colors come from traces of manganese within the mineral.

LEPIDOLITE

Lepidolite is an ore of lithium. The mineral also contains mica. Historically, thin sheets of mica have been used in electrical insulators and lampshades. Similarly, lepidolite comes in a layered structure. It has flexible sheets that return to their original shapes after bending. Lepidolite is usually lilac colored but can also have pink, yellow, or gray hues depending on its contents. It is a relatively soft mineral, ranking 2.5 to 4 on the Mohs scale.

Lithium is the lightest metal element. It is a critical component of batteries used for electric vehicles, smartphones, and cameras. Lithium also produces stronger ceramic and glass products.

CRITICAL MINING COPRODUCT

Most lepidolite is found in large-grained igneous rocks called pegmatites. Lepidolite can be found in small amounts around the globe. The mineral is typically collected while mining for other substances. Brazil is a producer of high-quality lepidolite used as gemstones. Lepidolite has also been found in several US states, including California and South Dakota.

Lepidolite-based lithium is used to make the rechargeable batteries in devices such as cell phones.

MUSCOVITE

Muscovite is the lightest-colored member of the mica mineral group. These minerals are known for their ability to split, or cleave, into thin, flexible sheets. Muscovite is usually clear, white, or silver. This allows light to pass through the mineral. Muscovite is very soft, ranking 2 to 2.5 on the Mohs scale.

EARLY GLASS SUBSTITUTE

People used muscovite for windowpanes before glass windowpanes became common. Today, heat-resistant muscovite is used to make fireplaces, ovens, and furnaces. The mineral is used to insulate electronic components too. This insulation helps regulate and direct electrical currents. Muscovite is a common additive in paints and coatings.

Muscovite is usually transparent or translucent with a pearly appearance.

It makes these products fire resistant. The mineral also adds sparkle to eye shadows and makeup highlighters.

Muscovite is found worldwide in igneous and metamorphic rocks. The largest muscovite crystal on record measured 16.4 by 9.8 feet (5 by 3 m). India, China, and Malawi are the top exporters of muscovite.

OLIVINE

Olivine is a rock-forming mineral that ranges from pale olive green to yellow green. The popular gemstone peridot comes from this mineral. Olivine is typically found within dark-colored igneous rocks. The hard mineral has a Mohs rating of 6.5 to 7. It is believed to be

Peridot from olivine has long been valued by many cultures worldwide. It is often associated with good luck.

the most common component of Earth's upper mantle, which is located between the crust and the interior core.

FERTILE VOLCANIC SOILS

Olivine is commonly found in ocean beds and in volcanic areas. The mineral's presence is one of the reasons that crops grow well in volcanic soils. This is because olivine weathers, or breaks down, on Earth's surface. The mineral releases iron and magnesium. These elements are important for plant growth. Olivine has been found in meteorites too. The mineral has limited industrial uses. But it has been valued as a gemstone since at least 1500 BCE.

Hawaii's Papakōlea Beach is one of only four green sand beaches in the world. The sand's unique color comes from olivine.

ORTHOCLASE

Orthoclase is a type of feldspar. It is one of the most abundant rock-forming minerals. Orthoclase gives many granites their pink color. But the mineral can also be colorless, white, cream, yellow, or brownish red. Orthoclase is the standard for the 6 rating on the Mohs scale.

Orthoclase can be found in many environments around the world. It begins as a component of igneous rocks. It can also be incorporated into sedimentary rocks when its grains separate from parent rocks. Some metamorphic rocks include orthoclase after igneous parent rocks undergo heat and pressure. The mineral has also been found in rock samples from the Moon and Mars.

Orthoclase is a type of potassium feldspar, or K-feldspar.

FOR FACTORIES AND JEWELRY BOXES

Glass and ceramics manufacturers use orthoclase to make dinnerware, glass, and building tiles. Orthoclase lowers the melting temperature needed for the production of these products. Orthoclase is used as an abrasive in cleaning products too. Gemstones also come from orthoclase. One is moonstone, which is valued for its moon-like glow.

Petalite was discovered in Sweden in 1800.

PETALITE

Petalite is a type of feldspar and an important source of lithium. A relatively durable mineral, petalite ranks 6.5 to 7 on the Mohs scale. It is often pearly white or colorless, but it can also include hints of pink and gray. Petalite is found around the world. It is often part of coarse-grained igneous rocks called pegmatites. Petalite commonly occurs beside lithium-bearing spodumene and lepidolite deposits. Australia is a leader in the mining of lithium-containing minerals.

ADDING STRENGTH, NOT WEIGHT

Soft, silvery lithium metal is used in many rechargeable batteries. It is in high demand because of its use in cell phones, laptops, and other electronics. Blending lithium with aluminum creates lighter, stronger metal alloys. These are used for airplanes, trains, and bicycle frames. Lithium is also found in glass, lubricants, and prescription drug compounds.

PHLOGOPITE

Phlogopite is a soft crystal that easily separates into thin, flexible, translucent sheets. Some phlogopite specimens are yellow brown or reddish brown in color. The mineral is usually found in marble-type rocks. Heat and pressure created it by altering existing sedimentary parent rocks.

HEAT-RESISTANT MATERIAL

Phlogopite and muscovite are the only mica minerals with significant commercial uses. Phlogopite is a poor conductor of heat and electrical currents. This makes it ideal for electronic circuit boards. This is because circuit boards are meant only to hold the pathways for electrical connections. It is important

Like other mica minerals, phlogopite has a low Mohs rating of 2 to 3.

that board materials themselves do not interfere with those connections. Phlogopite makes plastic automotive parts more durable too. It helps them resist temperature changes. Ground phlogopite can also be substituted for asbestos in brake linings. Adding phlogopite to industrial coatings helps them better withstand heat, chemicals, and sunlight.

Phlogopite can be mined in the form of sheets or flakes. Most sheets of mica originate in India. China and Finland are the world's leading producers of flake mica.

POLLUCITE

The rare mineral pollucite is an important source of cesium metal. Pollucite is almost always white or colorless. But sometimes it includes pink, violet, blue, or gray tints. The mineral is as hard as a steel nail.

Pollucite is commonly found within coarse-grained granite pegmatites. Large pollucite deposits have been discovered in Zimbabwe and Canada. One mine in Canada once held two-thirds of all easily accessible pollucite deposits.

HANDLE WITH CARE

Cesium is among the softest and most reactive metals. It melts at just over room temperature. The silver-gold metal is 70 times as abundant as silver. It occurs only in tiny quantities within

Cesium atoms all move at the same pace. Because of this, cesium plays a leading role in atomic clocks. These clocks set the standard for timekeeping around the world. Mobile phone, internet, and GPS systems all rely on them. Cesium-based clocks can be accurate to one second in 1.4 million years.

host minerals in Earth's crust. Cesium is useful for making precision lenses, mirrors, and prisms. It is used in drilling fluids for oil and gas wells and in radiation-monitoring equipment.

QUARTZ

Quartz is among the world's most widely used minerals. Most quartz crystals are clear or white. But impurities in the mineral can create different colors, such as purple, pink, gray, brown, and black. Quartz is harder than glass and most metals, rating 7 on the Mohs scale.

Quartz occurs worldwide in all three main rock types. These are igneous, sedimentary, and metamorphic rocks. It is the most commonly found mineral on mountaintops. It is also the primary component of sand. Its abundance and resistance to weathering make quartz readily available for human use. There are more names for variations of quartz than for any other mineral. Amethyst, agate, onyx, and flint are all types of quartz.

VERSATILE AND ABUNDANT

Ancient peoples once used quartz to make tools. Some of these tools, including arrowpoints, still exist. Today, quartz sand is used to make glass. It is used as an abrasive too. It is a flux in metalworking as well. Quartz sands can withstand the pressure needed to open

Pink-colored quartz is known as rose quartz. It is often used as a gemstone.

Quartz is a popular choice for kitchen countertops in homes. Quartz countertops come in a variety of patterns and colors.

oil and natural gas wells for drilling.

Today, most quartz is crushed and used as a sturdy base for building roads. It is also used in building construction for countertops, flooring, and wall decorations. China, India, and Brazil lead the world in quartz exports.

DID YOU KNOW?

Some dinosaurs swallowed stones to help digest plants. Paleontologists, or people who study fossils, call these stones gastroliths. Most stones broke down due to stomach acids in the dinosaurs' bodies. Only quartz gastroliths are known to have survived the digestive process.

SILICA

Silica is the main component of more than 95 percent of Earth's rocks. The mineral is a compound of the two most common elements on Earth, silicon and oxygen. The mass of Earth's crust is estimated to be 59 percent silica. The mineral ranks 7 on the Mohs scale. If there are no impurities present in silica, it appears clear.

Abundant and easily mined, silica is the primary ore of silicon. This substance is famously used in the semiconductors found in cell phones, laptops, and other electronic devices. Silicon has a melting point of 2,570 degrees

Fahrenheit (1,410°C). This makes it a popular refractory material for kilns and furnaces. Silicon is also used as an abrasive. It is part of glassmaking and paint production too.

FROM BUILDINGS TO PLAYGROUNDS

Silica sand is used as a flux in metalworking. It is used in water purification systems too. It is a common ingredient in concrete, mortar, bricks, and playground sand. Silica is found in many different environments around the globe. The United States and China lead the world in the production of sand and gravel. Both are common silica sources.

Silica sand is often extracted through open-pit mining, which involves extracting mineral deposits that are near Earth's surface.

SPODUMENE

Spodumene is an important source of lithium. It is known for its giant crystals. Spodumene crystals at South Dakota's Etta Mine commonly measure 3 to 4 feet (0.9 to 1.2 m) wide and 30 feet (9.1 m) long. The mineral can be found in many colors, including white, yellow, purple, blue, green, and pink. Spodumene is a hard mineral with a 6.5 to 7 Mohs rating.

Spodumene deposits often occur in coarse-grained pegmatites. It is common to find them beside the lithium ores petalite and lepidolite. Extracting lithium from these deposits is expensive. Most lithium is produced from lithium-rich waters below Earth's surface. These waters are primarily located in South America.

While spodumene has a high Mohs rating, it can split easily.

MORE ENERGY BY WEIGHT

Lithium was traditionally used for ceramic and glass production. It also works as a flux and lubricant. Today, the mineral is in high demand for use in rechargeable batteries. Lithium batteries offer more energy storage by weight than traditional lead-based or zinc-based batteries.

FINDING LITHIUM

Hard Rock Mining

- In hard rock mining, spodumene-containing rocks are crushed and ground into a powder. Leaching chemicals separate the lithium from other materials in the powder.
- The leaching chemicals are then filtered and treated with other chemicals to concentrate the lithium.
- This forces the lithium to precipitate, or turn into a solid. The solid lithium is filtered and dried.

Lithium evaporation ponds can range in color from bright blue to yellow. These colors come from varying amounts of lithium or salt.

Brine Extraction
• In brine extraction, lithium-rich liquids are pumped out of underground reservoirs and placed in evaporation ponds.
• The liquid in the ponds evaporates naturally over time, increasing the concentration of lithium in the brine.
• The evaporated brine solution is removed from the ponds. It is then treated with chemicals and filtered to extract the solid lithium.

Talc minerals are known for having a greasy, powdery texture.

TALC

Talc rates 1 on the Mohs scale, making it the softest mineral. Talc is also the name for many talc-containing rocks. The mineral is very common and can be found in shades of white, brown, gray, and green.

Most talc deposits occur in areas of major geological activity. These include places where mountains formed. Talc forms when geological processes involving heat and pressure change the contents of parent rocks.

MAKING BETTER PRODUCTS

Talc is often used in plastics to increase stiffness and improve heat resistance. It makes ceramics stronger too. When talc is added to paint, it brightens the paint's color and helps the paint stick to surfaces. In papermaking, talc can help fill gaps left by wood and other pulp materials. The mineral also makes paper whiter. Talc was once a common ingredient in cosmetics. The United States mines most of the talc it uses. China and India are leaders in global talc production.

Talc is often crushed into talcum powder, which is sometimes used in powder-based makeup products. The material is known for its ability to absorb moisture and oils.

TOURMALINE

Tourmalines are a group of minerals known for their broad array of colors. As a hard mineral with a Mohs rating of 7 to 7.5, tourmaline can withstand weathering. It can be found at the bottoms of riverbeds, in sediment deposits, and within sedimentary rocks.

Tourmaline has been used in pressure gauges and depth-sounder instruments inside military submarines.

Tourmaline is best known as a colorful gemstone. But it also has unique electrical properties. Some specimens generate an electrical charge when heated, cooled, or squeezed. This makes the minerals useful for detecting pressure changes. Researchers use tourmaline to help detect shock waves or underwater explosions. Tourmaline-based instruments can convert these pressure changes into measurable electrical signals.

HIGH-TEMPERATURE FORMATION

Tourmaline crystals typically begin as igneous-type rocks, such as granite or pegmatites. Hot, mineral-rich fluids penetrate crevices in the parent rocks and begin to circulate. Adding heat and pressure can cause changes in the composition of the parent rocks. This allows tourmaline crystals to form. Today, tourmaline is mined primarily in Brazil and Africa.

Some tourmalines have multiple colors. One popular variety is watermelon tourmaline, which features striking pink and green hues.

VERMICULITE

Vermiculites are a group of minerals known for their ability to expand when heated. Vermiculite is bronze to brownish yellow in color. It sometimes appears greenish. It is a soft mineral with a Mohs rating of just 1.5 to 2. Vermiculite can expand to roughly 30 times its original size. Expanded vermiculite can look like gold or grayish worms.

Vermiculite is lightweight and naturally fire resistant, making it useful as an insulating material. It can also absorb up to four times its weight in water. This makes the mineral useful in agricultural and potting soils. It is used to absorb spills too.

MINING VERMICULITE

Vermiculite is mined from deposits that have already heated and expanded. Before expanding, the mineral forms through the weathering of biotite or phlogopite. Vermiculite parent rocks often contain water molecules. This water is released under high temperatures. The United States is second only to South Africa in its volume of mined vermiculite.

ZEOLITES

Zeolites are a large group of useful minerals. They are found worldwide in igneous and sedimentary rocks. The crystal structure of zeolites includes water molecules that can escape as water vapor when heated. This gave the mineral its name, which means "boiling stone."

Zeolites can be colorless but also come in shades of white, yellow, pink, and red. The soft minerals, which rate 4 to 5 on the Mohs scale, can be crushed or powdered. Zeolite structures can function as filters. They filter, capture, and replace specific elements that move through them. This makes them useful in detergents, water filtration systems, and water

Scolecite is one type of zeolite mineral. It is known for its thin crystals.

softener systems. The same structure helps zeolites capture and hold liquids and odors. Zeolites are commonly used in cat litter. They are also used to remove heavy metals from farm fields. Slovakia and China are leaders in zeolite mining.

SYNTHETIC ZEOLITES

Zeolites are so useful that people have designed and produced synthetic versions of them. Natural zeolites vary in size and form. But synthetic zeolites can be created in uniform sizes for specific uses.

ZIRCON

Zircon is a relatively hard mineral that is found worldwide. Rating 6 to 7.5 on the Mohs scale, it is the primary ore of zirconium metal. Most zircon deposits originate in igneous rocks. Large zircon crystals can be found in some granites. But usually, zircon is found in the form of small, reddish-brown crystals. The mineral is common in stream gravels, beaches, and other sediment deposits. Its small size means it is often overlooked. Zircon crystals can be clear, gray, yellow, or blue.

HIGH-TEMPERATURE HERO

People have prized zircon as a gemstone for more than 2,000 years. The mineral has significant industrial applications too. It is valued for its heat-resistant and chemical-resistant properties.

Blue zircon is the most popular variety of the mineral. It is sometimes called starlite.

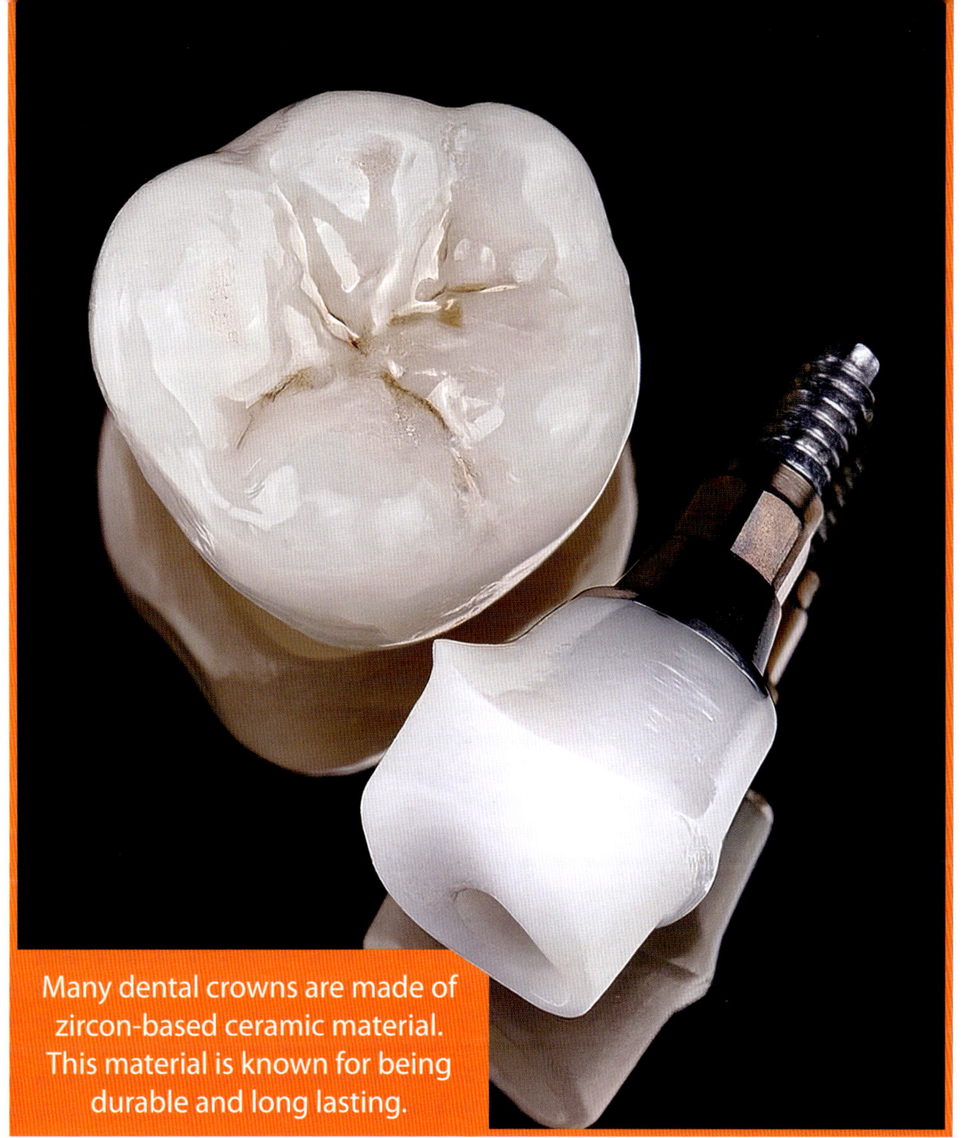

Many dental crowns are made of zircon-based ceramic material. This material is known for being durable and long lasting.

Factories use zircon to make production molds and other equipment used for high-temperature metal and ceramics production. Shiny gray zirconium is used to line fuel rods in nuclear reactors. Zirconium alloys have been used to build parts for jets and spacecraft. Zircon can also be heated to produce zirconium dioxide. People use this material to create durable dental crowns and implants. Australia leads the world in the production of industrial zircon.

ANHYDRITE

Anhydrite is a rock-forming mineral. It has the same chemical contents as gypsum but does not include water. Anhydrite is commonly found in thick layers alongside salt, gypsum, and limestone. It occurs in basins in which seawater has evaporated. The mineral can also form on shores or in tidal areas of salt water. Anhydrite can be colorless or white. It also comes in shades of gray, blue, pink, violet, and red. With a Mohs rating of 3 to 3.5, the mineral is slightly harder than gypsum.

ANHYDRITE IN INDUSTRY

Crushed anhydrite is used on farm fields to add calcium and sulfur to the soil. Plants use these minerals. When anhydrite is added to cement, it improves the material's strength and durability.

Angelite, a blue variety of anhydrite, was discovered in Peru in the 1980s.

The mineral is also used as a filler to make smoother, brighter paper. Paint and plastics manufacturers often add anhydrite to their compounds. This improves the compounds' texture and fire resistance. Anhydrite can be found worldwide. In the United States, anhydrite deposits are concentrated in Texas, Oklahoma, Louisiana, and New Mexico.

Barite sometimes forms into rose-like clusters in sand. These formations are called desert roses.

BARITE

Barite is an important ore of barium metal. This dense mineral sometimes appears white or colorless. Other times, it comes in light shades of green, red, blue, or yellow. Barite rates 2.5 to 3.5 on the Mohs scale. The mineral is often found in masses within sedimentary rocks. Barite can crystallize between grains of sand. It can grow into unique structures that meld sand and minerals into dense, sugary-looking clusters.

KEY TO STRONGER PRODUCTS

Barite is frequently used in oil and gas exploration. It adds heft to drilling muds. Drilling muds cool drill bits and move drill cuttings back up a well shaft. Barite is also added to rubber to make weighted mud flaps on vehicles. The mineral is added to the paper used to make playing cards so they are easier to shuffle. In medicine, barium can help block X-rays. Patients sometimes drink a barium liquid before one of these scans. The barium makes certain parts of the body show up more clearly. India, China, and Morocco are leading producers of barite.

Barite acts as a weighted filler between the paper fibers of playing cards. This makes the cards denser.

GYPSUM

Gypsum is a soft sulfate mineral. It can be found in the form of transparent crystals and white or gray masses. The mineral rates 2 on the Mohs scale. Gypsum forms through the evaporation of seawater or groundwater that contains dissolved sedimentary rock, such as limestone. Groundwater is water that is naturally stored underground.

Humans have used gypsum since ancient times. The ancient Egyptians used gypsum mortar to arrange the stones of their pyramids. The ancient Greeks used transparent gypsum crystals for windows before glass was invented. Today, gypsum remains a key ingredient in the cement and drywall used in modern construction. The mineral is an ideal building material because it easily loses, gains, and holds water. The moisture contained in drywall helps it reduce fire damage.

Farmers also use gypsum. They spread the mineral on fields to help the soil hold more moisture. Sidewalk chalk contains gypsum too. In the past,

Gypsum is similar to anhydrite. But unlike anhydrite, it contains water.

movie studios even used gypsum flakes as fake snow before computer-generated visuals were invented.

MINED IN THE USA

While gypsum can be found around the world, the United States is the world's leading producer of the mineral. The United States mines more than 20 million short tons (18.1 million metric tons) of gypsum annually. The average American home can also contain up to 7 short tons (6.4 metric tons) of gypsum.

SCHEELITE

The mineral scheelite is an ore of tungsten. It is typically white, yellow, brown, or green. The mineral can emit a bright blue or yellow glow under ultraviolet light. Scheelite has a Mohs rating of 4.5 to 5.

Scheelite is found in several geological environments. Most of the mineral formed when magma cooled and oozed into existing rock formations. These formations were then altered by hot, mineral-rich fluids. The fluids caused the rocks' composition to change. Today, leading

Scheelite is named after Swedish chemist Carl Wilhelm Scheele.

scheelite-producing nations include China, Vietnam,
and Russia.

MOST HEAT-RESISTANT METAL

Tungsten is a white or grayish metal that is used in alloys to
make harder, stronger steel. It is brittle at room temperature
but becomes highly flexible when heated. Tungsten has the
highest melting point of any metal. This led to its use as a lamp
filament material.

ARSENOPYRITE

Arsenopyrite is the most common ore of the semimetal arsenic. A semimetal is an element that has some metallic properties. While arsenic has some electrical conductivity, it doesn't have as much as true metals do. Arsenopyrite looks like a shiny, whitish-gray metal. It rates 5.5 to 6 on the Mohs scale.

Arsenopyrite is generally found in geological environments that have experienced very high temperatures. It can be an indicator mineral for gold and copper. Most arsenic is a by-product of the processing of other metals. China, Chile, and Morocco are the main producers of arsenic as a by-product.

BEYOND POISON

Naturally occurring arsenic is the twentieth most abundant element on Earth. It has been found in more than 760 types of minerals. Arsenic is best known as a poison. But it has many other uses too. Tiny amounts of arsenic are added to semiconductors such as silicon to improve their electrical conductivity. Arsenic can also help remove bubbles from glass. It helps protect wood from rot and insect damage too.

Arsenopyrite must be handled carefully due to its toxic qualities. Dust from the mineral can be dangerous or deadly if inhaled.

In the past, arsenic was a major ingredient in pesticides, herbicides, and insecticides.

DID YOU KNOW?

Miners used to test rocks for arsenic by hitting them with a pick or hammer. Arsenic-bearing rocks release a garlicky smell when hit.

BISMUTHINITE

Bismuthinite is the main source of ore for bismuth metal. It features metallic-gray or white crystals. The mineral is roughly as hard as a human fingernail. It is often found in veins within rocks. It forms when hot, bismuth-rich fluids circulate within the cracks of parent rocks.

METAL OF MANY USES

In the past, people often confused bismuth with lead. As early as the 1400s, bismuth was mixed with lead to make the metal letters used in old printing presses. Like lead, bismuth has a low melting point. Fire suppression systems use bismuth because it melts in hot air. This triggers a building's sprinkler systems before fires get too big. Bismuth is also good solder material because it swells slightly when it cools. The metal is an active ingredient in medicines for upset stomachs too. Most bismuth is produced as a by-product of lead processing. China, Laos, and South Korea produce most of the world's bismuth.

Fire sprinkler systems in public buildings often contain bismuth alloys. High heat melts the alloy and releases a water valve.

BORNITE

The brightly colored mineral bornite is also called peacock ore. This important ore of copper features shimmering blues, purples, golds, and greens. These bright colors come from surface tarnish and weathering. Today, bornite can be found around the globe. Chile leads the world in copper production. It is followed by the Democratic Republic of the Congo, Peru, China, and the United States.

Bornite typically forms when hot, mineral-rich fluids interact with existing rocks. The mineral forms within the cracks of parent rocks. Other times, it forms when existing minerals are altered. Bornite is a soft mineral that rates 3 on the Mohs scale.

Many mineral collectors value bornite for its iridescent luster and bright colors.

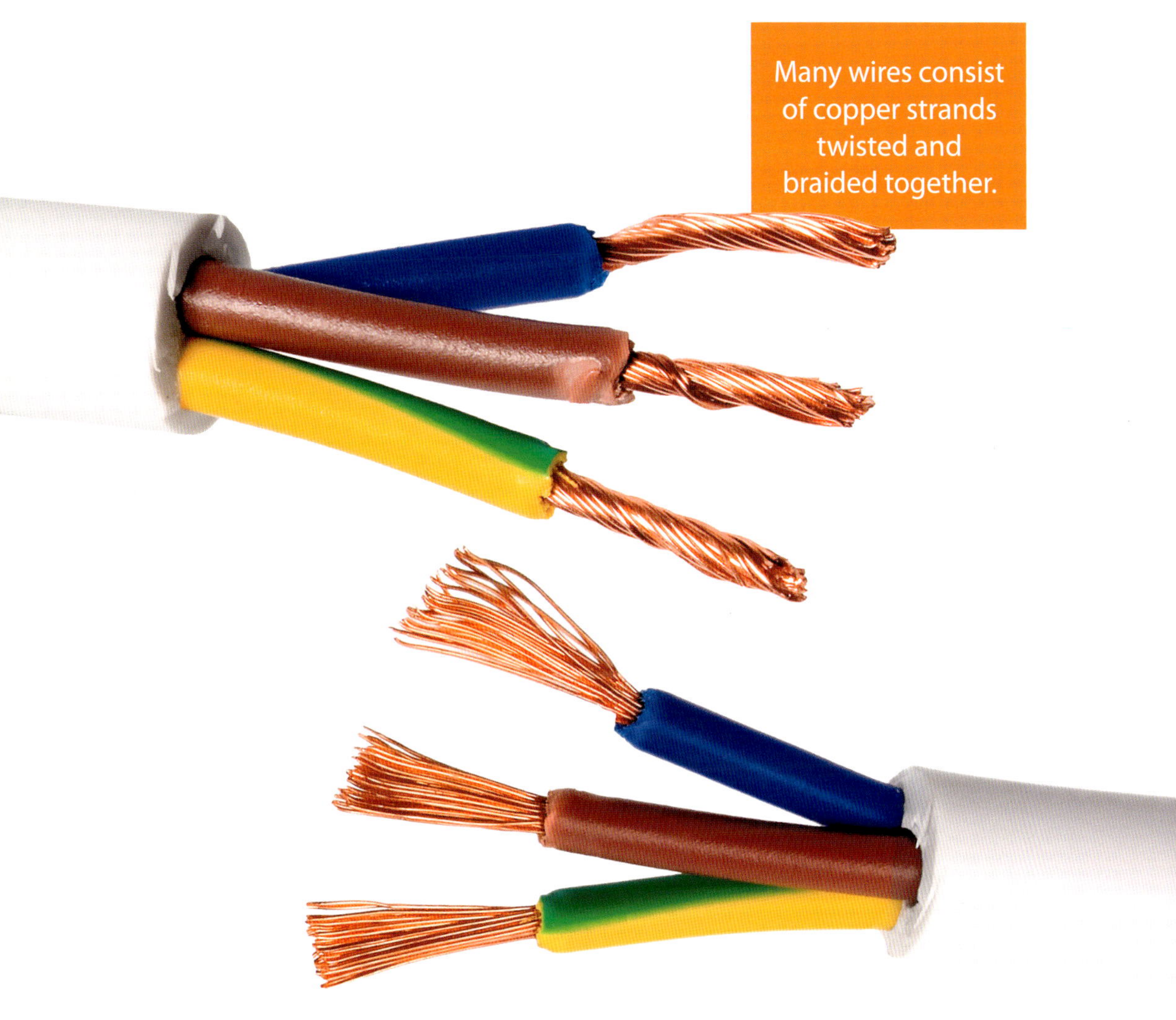

THE PERFECT CONDUCTOR

Copper is an excellent electrical conductor that is commonly used in wiring, motors, and electronics. An average car includes 50 pounds (23 kg) of copper. An average house includes 400 pounds (181 kg) of copper wiring, plumbing fixtures, and appliances. Copper piping was even used in ancient Egypt.

CALAVERITE

Calaverite is a rare mineral. It contains gold, the semimetal tellurium, and sometimes silver. Calaverite often appears yellow or yellowish white and has a Mohs rating of 2.5. The mineral can be found worldwide in small quantities. It typically forms when mineral-rich fluids flow through cracks in parent rocks.

Calaverite gets its name from Calaveras County, California, where it was first discovered.

RARE RESOURCE

Tellurium is a silvery-white element that has some but not all properties of a metal. It is less common than the REEs. Tellurium is used to boost the efficiency of solar panels. It is also used in copper, steel, and lead alloys to improve strength and flexibility. Most tellurium is a by-product of copper refining. China leads the world in the production of tellurium.

CHALCOPYRITE

Chalcopyrite is the most widely occurring ore of copper. This brassy yellow mineral can feature green, blue, or purple tarnishes. It is relatively soft, rating 3.5 to 4 on the Mohs scale. But it can also be brittle. Chalcopyrite is often found alongside the sulfide mineral pyrite. Both minerals are frequently mistaken for gold.

Chalcopyrite can be found in all three major rock types. It is often concentrated in veins. Veins develop when mineral-rich waters seep into the cracks of a parent rock. Chalcopyrite itself can be a source of secondary copper minerals. These include malachite and azurite. Chile leads the world in the production of copper from chalcopyrite, followed by the Democratic Republic of the Congo, Peru, China, and the United States.

To tell chalcopyrite and gold apart, people can compare the minerals' streaks. Chalcopyrite leaves behind a greenish-black streak, while gold makes a yellow streak.

POWERING THE BRONZE AGE

Humans have been using copper for more than 6,000 years. They used it to create tools and weapons during the Bronze Age (3000–1000 BCE). Today, copper is used for electrical wiring and other electronic components because of its high conductivity and resistance to corrosion.

COBALTITE

Cobaltite is a shiny mineral that ranges from silver gray to white in color. It typically forms when mineral-rich fluids deposit minerals in parent rocks. Cobaltite is one of several minerals that is mined for cobalt, a distinctive blue metal. With a 5.5 Mohs rating, cobaltite is considered a medium-hard mineral.

Cobaltite minerals sometimes feature cube-shaped crystals.

Cobaltite can be found around the world. Most industrial cobalt is produced as a by-product of copper and nickel processing. The Democratic Republic of the Congo leads the world in cobalt production. The nation's cobalt production industry has been investigated for human rights abuses such as child labor.

GREEN ENERGY WONDER

Cobalt is an important metal for modern lifestyles. It adds strength and heat to alloys while making them more resistant to corrosion. The metal is also a critical element in lithium-ion batteries, which are used in electric vehicles and portable electronics. Cobalt is used in magnets that help solar panels and wind turbines convert sunlight and wind into electricity. Cobalt is nonreactive with human tissue too. This means it can be used in medical and dental implants.

MINING AND THE ENVIRONMENT

Mining is important for clean energy, consumer products, and the global economy. But it also contributes to water pollution, habitat loss, deforestation, and erosion. It has been tied to human rights abuses and safety hazards for workers too. In 2023, 40 miners died in mining accidents in the United States. Roughly 2,000 cobalt miners die each year in the Democratic Republic of the Congo. More than 15 percent of those miners are children. Governments around the world work to address these problems. Mining companies aim to reduce their water and energy use. New precision drilling techniques can help reduce mining's effects. Consumers can help by recycling electronics, batteries, and other products whenever possible.

COOPERITE

The metallic-gray mineral cooperite is one of several platinum-bearing minerals. Minerals that contain platinum tend to be found in places that experience the shifting of tectonic plates. Cooperite and other minerals can be collected from streambeds and other areas in which minerals mix with sand and gravel. Cooperite rates 4 to 5 on the Mohs scale.

A SPECIAL METAL

Platinum is among the rarest metals on Earth. It is used primarily in vehicles' catalytic converters, which help reduce pollution from exhaust. The metal is also valued in chemical manufacturing for its ability to speed up chemical reactions.

Cooperite is named after Richard A. Cooper. In 1928, he discovered the mineral in South Africa.

Platinum's excellent electrical conductivity and resistance to corrosion make it useful in many electronics. Today, South Africa is the world's leading producer of platinum.

GALENA

Galena is the most important ore of lead. Its heavy, metallic-gray crystals split easily into cubes. The mineral is about as hard as a human fingernail. It is a common vein mineral. Vein minerals are created by mineral-rich fluids flowing through the cracks of existing rocks. Galena is typically found alongside other metal ore minerals such as pyrite, sphalerite, and chalcopyrite.

A TOXIC LEGACY

Lead is a soft metal that humans have used for more than 8,000 years. Pipes, paints, and ceramic glazes once included lead. The metal has been used as a gasoline additive too. Research on lead's toxicity led to the metal being discontinued in most products. Modern manufacturers use lead mostly in batteries and as a radiation shield to protect patients during X-rays. Today, most galena mining takes place in Australia, Sweden, and Idaho. The mineral is often mined at the same time as zinc, copper, and silver.

Galena minerals are dense and tend to be heavy for their size.

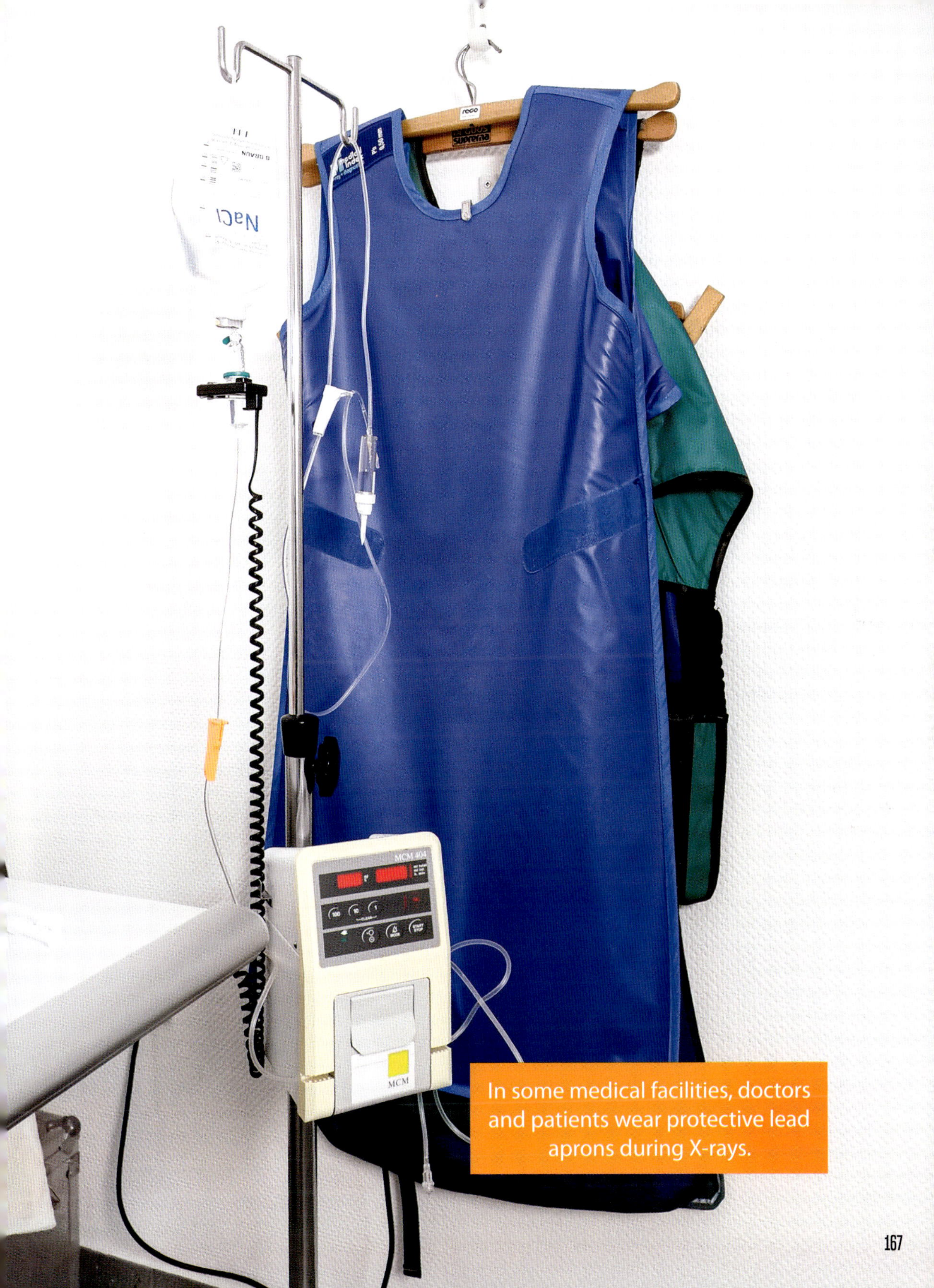

In some medical facilities, doctors and patients wear protective lead aprons during X-rays.

MOLYBDENITE

The greasy mineral molybdenite is often dark gray, bluish, or silver in color. It is an important source of the metal molybdenum. Molybdenite is among the softest minerals. Many people originally thought it was lead. Today, molybdenite is found worldwide. It usually forms in areas that have experienced extreme geological events such as the clashing of tectonic plates.

HEAT-TOLERANT ALLOYS

Molybdenum is often added to steel and other metals to improve

Molybdenite rates 1 to 1.5 on the Mohs scale.

Molybdenum is often used in steel cutting tools such as saws and drills.

their strength. It makes metal alloys more resistant to heat and corrosion too. The melting point of molybdenum is much higher than that of steel. This makes the metal ideal for rocket engines, cutting tools, and electric filaments. Most molybdenum is a by-product of copper mining. China, Chile, and the United States are major molybdenum producers.

ORPIMENT

Orpiment is a beautiful, toxic mineral with a long history. It comes in shades of vibrant lemon yellow, gold, and warm brown. Orpiment typically forms when hot fluids that are rich in arsenic and sulfur flow through cracks and gaps in rocks. Orpiment crystals begin to form as the minerals in the water become more concentrated. Volcanic rocks, hot springs, and geothermal areas may contain orpiment. The soft mineral rates just 1.5 to 2 on the Mohs scale.

GOLDEN AND TOXIC

Artists in ancient Egypt and China used orpiment as a yellow pigment. Healers believed orpiment could treat diseases such as malaria. Ancient Egyptians used the mineral to kill insects and weeds. Some people thought orpiment could be turned into gold because the two minerals looked similar.

Orpiment contains arsenic. Once people realized the mineral was toxic, its use as a pigment declined. The mineral is often found near gold, which gives it value as a mineral indicator. Many mineral collectors still value orpiment. Significant orpiment deposits have been found in Romania, Peru, Japan, and the United States.

PENTLANDITE

Pentlandite is among the most important ores of nickel. It comes in shades of pale yellow, bronze, and brown. The mineral is a primary component of parent rocks formed by nickel-rich magma from Earth's mantle. As the magma cools, pentlandite collects and creates high-grade nickel. Pentlandite is about as hard as a penny. It often intergrows with pyrrhotite, another nickel-bearing mineral.

Silvery, corrosion-resistant nickel is commonly used to make coins. People alloyed nickel with zinc as early as 200 BCE. Early humans sometimes found easily accessible iron and nickel in meteorites, which they combined to make stronger, more rust-resistant metal. Nickel continues to add longevity and durability to other metals. Modern toaster manufacturers use nickel because it resists rust even when it gets very hot. Facilities that remove salt from salt water rely on nickel components to resist saltwater corrosion.

Pentlandite was first found in Sudbury, Ontario, Canada. Joseph Barclay Pentland discovered it.

ONE OF EARTH'S CORE METALS

Geologists believe that nickel and iron make up most of Earth's core. Nickel is also very common in meteorites. Because of this, geologists believe that the metal is a common element on other planets too. Today, pentlandite is mined primarily in Canada, Russia, Australia, and South Africa.

ARTIFICIAL INTELLIGENCE IN MINING

Artificial intelligence (AI) is making mining safer and more efficient. Mining companies are using autonomous vehicles to haul material from mines to processing facilities. In-mine robots can operate around the clock and reach places that humans cannot. AI-based sorting systems can spot and recover valuable materials missed by humans. AI's greatest contribution is its ability to discover patterns in huge amounts of data. This helps mining companies make more accurate predictions about where to look for minerals. Sophisticated weather prediction systems alert miners to potential dangers from wildfires and storms.

Pyrite crystals can take many different forms, including cube-shaped clusters.

PYRITE

Pyrite is a metallic-yellow mineral. Its name comes from a Greek phrase that means "stone that strikes fire." The mineral creates sparks when struck against hard surfaces, which helped early humans start fires. Known as "fool's gold," pyrite looks similar to gold. But with a Mohs rating of 6 to 6.5, the mineral is much harder than gold.

Pyrite forms in environments that are rich with sulfur and iron and low in oxygen. The mineral is found in all three main rock types. Pyrite often forms when mineral-rich fluids flow into cracks in rocks and cool. The mineral can be found in coal deposits and near mineral ores of gold, copper, lead, and zinc.

MINERAL CLUES

Pyrite's sulfur content can be extracted to make chemicals used in factories, farms, and households. Pyrite is also an important indicator mineral for valuable mineral deposits. Geologists study pyrite to learn more about past geological events.

PYRRHOTITE

Pyrrhotite is a minor source of nickel and the only bronze-colored magnetic mineral. It is typically found in igneous rocks alongside pyrite and quartz. Pyrrhotite is a medium-hard mineral that contains iron and sulfur. People once mined it for iron. But they stopped after cheaper, sulfur-free iron sources were discovered. Today, pyrrhotite is still mined for nickel if it contains a high enough percentage of the metal.

CONSTRUCTION MYSTERY

In the past, pyrrhotite-rich rocks were commonly crushed and used in concrete in places where the mineral was abundant.

Pyrrhotite is sometimes called magnetic pyrite.

But much of the concrete started crumbling and cracking. Researchers discovered that pyrrhotite expands when exposed to air and water. The US Geological Survey informed construction companies about the problem and worked with them to find alternatives.

Realgar often forms in prism-shaped crystals.

REALGAR

Beautiful and deadly, realgar is an ore of arsenic semimetal. It is often red or orange in color. The mineral's bright, transparent crystals led to its nickname: ruby sulfur. Chemically, realgar is very similar to orpiment. Both minerals can be found near Earth's surface around hot springs and geothermal vents.

BRILLIANT RED

Realgar's vibrant color made it a favorite pigment of ancient artists. Ancient Chinese healers believed the mineral had

medicinal powers. Realgar was often found near gold, which made some people believe it could be turned into gold itself. Once people realized that realgar was toxic, it was used mainly to kill weeds and insects. Today, modern manufacturers use less-toxic alternatives.

Realgar is found around the globe. China, the United States, and Russia have significant deposits of the mineral. However, realgar is not commonly mined due to its toxicity. It also breaks down into pararealgar, a yellow-orange powder, when exposed to sunlight over time.

Realgar was once used in fireworks.

The town of Skotterud, Norway, gives skutterudite its name.

SKUTTERUDITE

Skutterudite is an ore of cobalt and nickel that ranges from silver gray to white in color. It is roughly as hard as glass. Skutterudite is generally found in the cracks or fractures of rocks that were filled by hot, metal-rich fluids. It can also be found alongside other cobalt-bearing and nickel-bearing minerals.

THERMOELECTRIC STAR

Skutterudite was originally mined for cobalt and nickel. But modern scientists now study skutterudite as a thermoelectric material. These are materials that convert heat into electricity. Skutterudite is unusual because it conducts heat like a metal and heats up like glass. These features may help the mineral capture waste heat produced by factories and vehicles. Skutterudite was first found in Norway. Canada and the United States are also home to significant skutterudite deposits.

NASA is studying the
use of skutterudite
in thermoelectric
generators, which are
used in spacecraft.

SPERRYLITE

The rare mineral sperrylite is a major ore of platinum. It is roughly as hard as a steel nail. Sperrylite appears as single or clustered bluish-white or silver cubes. It is usually found within rocks that originated deep within Earth's mantle. These ore-rich rocks form giant layers as they rise to Earth's surface through tectonic forces.

MILES OF MINERALS

South Africa is home to one such layered rock formation. The Bushveld Igneous Complex is nearly 230 miles (370 km) long. It is home to 70 percent of all known platinum resources. Copper, nickel, and chromite are found in the complex too.

Platinum is used primarily in catalytic converters. The metal is also included in some drug compounds that are used to treat certain cancers. Doctors believe the platinum compounds bond with cancer cells, preventing them from creating more cancer cells.

Sperrylite has a Mohs rating of 6 to 7 and is known for its metallic luster.

Many mines are located in the Bushveld Igneous Complex. These include platinum, chromium, tin, fluorite, and titanium mines.

SPHALERITE

Sphalerite is a combination of iron and zinc. It is the most important ore of zinc. Its varying iron content creates a spectrum of colors. Sphalerite can be yellow, blue, or green. It can also be red, brown, or black. Sphalerite frequently contains smaller amounts of gallium, germanium, and indium. These elements are used in electronics, solar panels, LED lights, and alloys. Sphalerite is about as hard as a penny.

People have used silver-white zinc since the Middle Ages, beginning in about 500 CE. While zinc tarnishes, it resists rust.

Sphalerite is sometimes called blende or zinc blende.

Many steel and iron parts used in cars, streetlights, and bridges are covered with zinc. This helps prevent rust and wear. A zinc product called zinc oxide is used to whiten paints. It also helps painted surfaces resist rust and mildew. Zinc oxide in sunscreen protects human skin by reflecting ultraviolet rays.

MINING

Sphalerite is found worldwide in sedimentary deposits and geothermal vents. It is often found near galena. Because of this, early miners sought lead within sphalerite's crystals. Today, China is the leading producer of zinc.

Zinc oxide sunscreens do not absorb into skin. Instead, they create a protective barrier on the skin, blocking harmful rays of sunlight.

STIBNITE

Stibnite, which is shiny, soft, and silvery, is the primary ore of the semimetal antimony. Antimony originates in molten liquids deep below Earth's surface. Stibnite is created via hydrothermal deposits or epithermal veins. Epithermal veins form in parent rocks at lower temperatures closer to Earth's surface. Stibnite deposits are relatively common around the world.

FROM BULLETS TO BATTERIES

Antimony is used in alloys to create harder, stronger metals. During World War II (1939–1945), the US military used antimony to make sturdier bullets. Modern uses for the semimetal include flame retardants and batteries. Antimony has been studied for use in cheaper, longer-lasting liquid-metal batteries. Unlike in solid batteries, liquid battery components do not break down during charging and discharging. China, Tajikistan, and Russia are leaders in antimony production.

During World War II, antimony was used to harden lead ammunition and make tungsten steel. These materials were important for the war effort.

GLOSSARY

catalytic
Able to speed up chemical reactions without degrading or being used up in the process.

compound
A substance made by combining two or more chemical elements together.

conductor
A material that allows electricity or heat to move through it easily.

deposit
A natural collection of a material, often formed by natural processes.

element
A basic substance that cannot be broken down into anything simpler.

evaporation
The process of changing from a liquid to a vapor or gas.

flux
A substance that helps things melt or join together or that removes unwanted materials.

geologist
A person who studies the structure, makeup, and history of Earth.

hydrothermal
Involving hot water from underground.

igneous
Describing rocks that form when magma cools down and solidifies.

mantle
The thick layer of melted rock between Earth's crust and its core.

metamorphic
Describing rocks that change in composition due to high heat and pressure underground.

prism
A three-dimensional shape with two identical, parallel faces connected by sides.

sedimentary
Describing rocks that form when layers of sediment, or minerals and organic matter carried by water, are compressed over time.

synthetic
Something made by humans instead of naturally made.

tarnish
A chemical change that affects the surface of a mineral.

tectonic
Of or relating to the way giant rock pieces, or plates, move around and against one another to change Earth's surface.

FURTHER READINGS

Bell, Samantha S. *The Crystal and Gemstone Encyclopedia*. Abdo, 2026.

Dennie, Devin. *An Anthology of Rocks and Minerals*. DK, 2024.

Rock & Gem: The Definitive Guide to Rocks, Minerals, Gems, and Fossils. DK, 2023.

ONLINE RESOURCES

To learn more about minerals, please visit **abdobooklinks.com** or scan this QR code. These links are routinely monitored and updated to provide the most current information available.

PHOTO CREDITS

Cover Photos: Albert Russ/Shutterstock Images, front (fluorite), back (tourmaline, stibnite); Marcel Clemens/Shutterstock Images, front (gold); Shutterstock Images, front (corundum, hemimorphite, quartz, barite, scheelite, orpiment); Minakryn Ruslan/Shutterstock Images, front (spinel, kyanite); Bjoern Wylezich/Shutterstock Images, front (torbernite); Alejandro Lafuente Lopez/Shutterstock Images, back (pyrite)

Interior Photos: Shutterstock Images, 1, 5, 7, 8, 9, 17 (talc), 17 (apatite), 17 (quartz), 17 (diamond), 20, 22, 24, 26–27, 27, 28, 30, 34, 35 (bottom), 37, 39, 40, 41, 47, 49, 50, 53, 54, 55 (paint), 56–57, 60, 62–63, 63, 73, 82, 87, 91, 93 (bottom), 96, 103, 104, 107, 109, 111, 112, 112–113, 115, 121, 123, 125, 126, 128, 131, 132–133, 135, 136, 139, 140, 141, 142, 143, 144, 145, 150, 150–151, 157, 163, 165, 167, 170, 179; Richard Leeney/Dorling Kindersley RF/Getty Images, 3; Ralf Lehmann/Shutterstock Images, 6; Red Line Editorial, 11; Bteu/Tekniska/Alamy, 12; John Cancalosi/Alamy, 13; Dorling Kindersley Ltd./Alamy, 14; Alexander Oganezov/Shutterstock Images, 15; Sheila Fitzgerald/Shutterstock Images, 16; Kazakov Maksim/Shutterstock Images, 17 (calcite); Athanasios Gioumpasis/Getty Images News/Getty Images, 18–19; Alejandro Lafuente Lopez/Shutterstock Images, 19, 57, 174; Halit Omer/Shutterstock Images, 21; Jon G. Fuller, Jr./VW Pics/Universal Images Group/Getty Images, 23; Albert Russ/Shutterstock Images, 25, 48, 86, 137, 160, 178–179, 180, 186; Andriy Kananovych/Shutterstock Images, 29; John Holst/Shutterstock Images, 30–31; Marcel Clemens/Shutterstock Images, 32, 148; Photo Researchers/Science History Images/Alamy, 33; Constantine Pankin/Shutterstock Images, 35 (top); Sebastian Janicki/Shutterstock Images, 36; PB/YB/Alamy, 38, 51, 92, 93 (top), 100, 158–159, 164; Fokin Oleg/Shutterstock Images, 42; Marcus Yam/Los Angeles Times/Getty Images, 43; Monty Rakusen/DigitalVision/Getty Images, 44; Dirk Wiersma/Science Source, 45, 64, 74; lissart/E+/Getty Images, 46; José María Barres Manuel/Alamy, 52; Arndt Vladimir/iStockphoto, 55 (brushes); ViewStock/Getty Images, 58; Vitaly Raduntsev/Shutterstock Images, 59; Janek Skarzynski/AFP/Getty Images, 60–61; Javi Sanz/E+/Getty Images, 65; Shevelev Alexey/Shutterstock Images, 66; Max Mumby/Indigo/Getty Images Entertainment/Getty Images, 67; DEA/R. Appiani/De Agostini/Getty Images, 68; Iuliia Bondar/Moment/Getty Images, 69; De Agostini Picture Library/Getty Images, 70; Mondadori Portfolio/Getty Images, 70–71; David G. Hayes/Shutterstock Images, 72; George Rose/Getty Images Entertainment/Getty Images, 75; GC Minerals/Alamy, 76–77; Bjoern Wylezich/Shutterstock Images, 77, 97, 98, 116, 168, 184; Norman Posselt/fStop/Getty Images, 78; Maxal Tamor/Shutterstock Images, 79; Matteo Chinellato/Alamy, 80; Natural History Museum, London/Alamy, 81; The Natural History Museum, London/Science Source, 83, 162, 183; Phil Degginger/Jack Clark Collection/Science Source, 84; Maksim Safaniuk/Shutterstock Images, 85; SunChan/E+/Getty Images, 88; Ryan McFadden/MediaNews Group/Reading Eagle/Getty Images, 89; Tyler Boyes/Shutterstock Images, 90; Michael Andrew Just/Shutterstock Images, 94; Athima Tongloom/Moment/Getty Images, 95; ferrantraite/E+/Getty Images, 99; Samunella/Alamy, 101; Nick Knight/Shutterstock Images, 102; Oliver Berg/dpa/picture alliance/Getty Images, 105; United States Geological Survey, 106; Aleksandr Pobedimskiy/Shutterstock Images, 108; Moha El-Jaw/Shutterstock Images, 110; Valery Voennyy/Alamy, 114; Damien Verrier/Shutterstock Images, 116–117; Phil Degginger/Science Source, 118; Gidofalvi Kinga-Kamilla/Shutterstock Images, 119; Henri Koskinen/Shutterstock Images, 120, 130; Tom Grundy/Alamy, 122; SBS Eclectic Images/Alamy, 124; Sheila Say/Shutterstock Images, 127; Juan Enrique del Barrio/Shutterstock Images, 129; Diego Sugoniaev/Shutterstock Images, 134; Ton Ponchai/Shutterstock Images, 138; Ingrid Rousseau/Shutterstock Images, 146; Arnik Pratama/Shutterstock Images, 147; Tatiana Gordievskaia/Shutterstock Images, 149; Minakryn Ruslan/Shutterstock Images, 152; Fox Photos/Hulton Archive/Getty Images, 153, 187; Harry Taylor/Dorling Kindersley/Science Source, 154, 176; Sanit Fuangnakhon/Shutterstock Images, 155; Stefan Malloch/Shutterstock Images, 156; Charles D. Winters/Science Source, 159; DEA Picture Library/De Agostini/Getty Images, 161; Marco Fine/Shutterstock Images, 166; Akimov Igor/Shutterstock Images, 168–169; Vadim Petrakov/Shutterstock Images, 171; Phil Degginger/Alamy, 172; Douglas Sacha/Moment/Getty Images, 173; Michael LaMonica/Shutterstock Images, 175; imageBROKER.com/Alamy, 177; NASA/JPL-Caltech/Science History Images/Alamy, 180–181; GS International/Greenshoots Communications/Alamy, 182–183; Keith Homan/Shutterstock Images, 185

ABDOBOOKS.COM

Published by Abdo Reference, a division of ABDO, PO Box 398166, Minneapolis, Minnesota 55439. Copyright © 2026 by Abdo Consulting Group, Inc. International copyrights reserved in all countries. No part of this book may be reproduced in any form without written permission from the publisher. Encyclopedias™ is a trademark and logo of Abdo Reference.

Printed in China.
082025
012026

Editor: Laura Stickney
Series Designer: Colleen McLaren
Production Designer: Ebonee Estrella

LIBRARY OF CONGRESS CONTROL NUMBER: 2025939303

PUBLISHER'S CATALOGING-IN-PUBLICATION DATA

Names: Wheeler, Jill C., author.
Title: The mineral encyclopedia / by Jill C. Wheeler
Description: Minneapolis, Minnesota: Abdo Reference, 2026 | Series: Geology encyclopedias | Includes online resources and index.
Identifiers: ISBN 9781098298906 (lib. bdg.) | ISBN 9798384932703 (ebook)
Subjects: LCSH: Minerals--Juvenile literature. | Rocks--Juvenile literature. | Rock minerals--Juvenile literature. | Geology--Juvenile literature. | Encyclopedias--Juvenile literature.
Classification: DDC 552--dc23